The Journey to Prison . . . is ar. ...., rather than an expert, opinion. It's thoughtful, it's emotive, it's interesting and it's easy to digest. Ces Lashlie is a woman of compassion, humanity, and refreshing candour, and people who read this book will not fail to find enrichment in the counsel it offers. *New Zealand Books*

Lashlie writes with modesty and common sense.
Waikato Times

Not a comfortable book, but one to be read by everyone who feels New Zealand society is breaking down.
The Star

Perceptive and straight-talking . . . It should be required reading. *The Daily News*

This thought-provoking book is sure to challenge readers' views. *Timaru Herald*

A readable account that will better inform both sides of the argument. *Wanganui Chronicle*

A short, frightening book we should all be reading from cover to cover. *Daily Post*

[A] reader-friendly, perceptive and blunt-speaking book.
Manawatu Evening Standard

CELIA LASHLIE

THE JOURNEY TO PRISON
Who goes and why

REVISED EDITION

HarperCollins*Publishers*

National Library of New Zealand Cataloguing-in-Publication Data

Lashlie, Celia.
The journey to prison : who goes and why / Celia Lashlie. Rev. ed.
Previous ed.: 2002.
ISBN 1-86950-474-7
1. Crime—Sociological aspects—New Zealand. 2. Criminal behavior—
New Zealand. 3. Prisoners—New Zealand. I. Title.
364.993—dc 21

This edition first published 2003
Reprinted 2004
HarperCollins*Publishers (New Zealand) Limited*
P.O. Box 1, Auckland

ISBN 1 86950 474 7
Designed and typeset by Chris O'Brien
Printed by Griffin Press, Australia on 79 gsm Bulky Paperback

For Rebekah and Gene, who have led me to know myself
and taught me about joy.

For those who have walked with me on the journey of life
and taught me about love.

And, for the women in prison in New Zealand, who made me
laugh and taught me about courage.

For the Rochdale

Youth Offending Team,

Warm regards,

Celia.

PUROTU
seeking the magic

The purotu symbol was designed for me by Heather Busch, a good friend of mine, after discussions focused on the ability of people who have experienced tragedy and trauma to 'fly' if given the chance. Used as an adjective, the Maori word 'purotu' means clear or transparent, and when he was working with the women of Christchurch Women's Prison, Jim Moriarty used it to refer to 'the pure place within'. In Heather's design the jagged curve is the negative history and trauma people bring into prison with them. If prisons do what they are equipped to do, and do it well, the individual will leave grounded in their history, aware of the victims they have created, but also convinced of their ability to do it differently from this point. As depicted in the purotu symbol, upon leaving prison they soar, having discovered their own magic, having visited the pure place within and knowing the positive contribution they are capable of making to our society.

Contents

Introduction

Who goes to prison in this country? When you hear the words *prison inmate*, what image drifts into your mind? Is it the tattooed face of a gang member or the face of one of the high-profile violent offenders we regularly see featured in the television news? What do you believe about the people who make it to prison? In your view, do they end up in prison by accident or have they consciously chosen to be there, having deliberately broken the law? Who are they and why are they there? Perhaps more importantly, what has it got to do with us — you and me?

The images portrayed in the media in relation to prisons and prison inmates leave us with the impression that they are places filled with dangerous people, people who deserve to be there, people who have deliberately committed a vicious crime and forfeited their right to live in our communities. We repeatedly hear the view that if only prisons were tougher, if only prison staff didn't feed the inmates quite so well, worked them harder and took the time to remind them at least once a day that they were worthless human beings, then inmates serving their time in these most desolate of places would choose not to return. And thus the crime problem would be solved. It's an appealing idea for a society struggling to come to terms with what it means to know city streets are no longer safe, doors to vehicles and houses must now be locked and personal freedom is not what it used to be in the clean green paradise we call home.

The current approach taken to social justice issues in New

Zealand appears to be one of assigning blame and then seeking to move the perceived problem to somewhere just outside our stream of consciousness. We tell ourselves that those who are in prison deserve to be there and we seek to ensure they stay there as long as possible. Having told ourselves, in the face of yet another violent murder or home invasion, that New Zealand is a paradise, providing opportunities for all who want to make something of themselves and a great place to raise children, we reassure ourselves there is nothing we can, or even ought to do, other than make prison as unpleasant an experience as possible, to ensure those who make it there choose not to return when they are released.

The hard-to-digest reality is that people who come to prison come from our communities — yours and mine. Their journey to prison often began on the day they were born and has been prompted not by their evil nature or any innate tendency to commit crime, but rather by the simple reality that they have had the misfortune to be born into the 'wrong' family.

In classrooms around New Zealand, right now, there are a number of children whose destiny is already in place — unless a miracle occurs in their life, they will come to prison and the chances are high they will have killed or seriously maimed someone in the course of their journey to the prison gates. And the age of these children? It would be a serious enough concern if the answer to that question was 17 or 18 years of age, the 'stuff' of rebellious adolescence and children whose desire to experience life fully means they don't stop to think until the concrete walls of a police cell detain them.

Unfortunately, the children I am thinking of are nowhere near their seventeenth birthday. It is true there are children of that age who are well on their way into prison, but the children I am thinking of are currently only 5, 6 and 7 years of age. They are children who occupy the thoughts of their teachers as they try to change the destiny already visible; children who will struggle every moment of their life simply because of the reality into which they were born; children who form part of a lost generation many New Zealanders are doing their very best to ignore. In fact, not only are we trying to ignore them, we are beginning to actively avoid them and the issues they raise.

A disturbing trend in recent months has been the degree to which any community 'threatened' with the idea of a prison or a youth justice facility being built in their area has mobilised itself to ensure the idea does not gain ground. Where are we to build the facilities needed to contain these children when the inevitable happens and they do offend? Anywhere but in our back yards, it would seem.

So where does the idea of a 5-year-old already on his or her way into prison fit in a justice system built on the idea that they would choose not to come if they were frightened enough by the reality that is prison? And what consolation does it offer to the parents and family of the person yet to be killed by the same 5-year-old to know that when that child finally arrives in prison, having killed someone they love, the law will move to see them detained there for a long time?

It *is* true that some people need to be detained for a very long time, possibly even for the term of their natural life, but they are a very small minority in a prison population currently numbering around 5500 and climbing.

As the world around us grows more violent and less understandable, our need for vengeance and revenge seems to be growing at a comparable rate. The challenging reality we might have to face, if we are serious about making a difference for our children and grandchildren and turning the tide of increasing societal violence, is that until we stop shifting the blame and looking for instant solutions and work instead on finding the courage to deal with the issues in a holistic way, nothing will change.

Horrifying though it may be, the reality is that many of those currently in prison were predestined to come from a very early age, and a significant number of children currently in our schools are already on their way. The stories of those who have walked the path to prison contain many of the answers we need if we are to begin to make a real difference, rather than continuing with the current practice of simply papering over the cracks. The question for us all is whether we have the courage to listen with an open mind to the stories of the people in prison — to hear what needs to be heard and begin the process of truly understanding the connections that have influenced their journey.

It is not about seeking to excuse, it is about seeking to *understand* in order to learn. Only through understanding will we begin the process of identifying real solutions to real problems and come to know the part we all can, and must, play in order to make a difference.

As you begin this book, know that it does not contain the answers. Rather it seeks to identify the questions and outline the issues from one person's perspective — my own. I haven't written this book because I believe the views I hold have any greater validity than yours, but because I believe that only through robust debate will we find our way to effective responses to the increasing levels of crime and violence so clearly evident within our society.

This book seeks to contribute to the debate, providing an alternative perspective to the one that suggests sending people to prison for longer and making prisons more uncomfortable will somehow see the problems we are currently facing resolved.

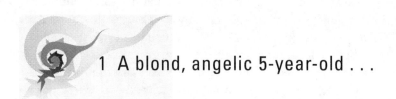

1 A blond, angelic 5-year-old . . .

At about 8.15 a.m. on Thursday 19 April 2001, I received a phone call from a Radio New Zealand producer, asking if I was willing to be interviewed on the *Kim Hill Show* later that morning. I was surprised by the call and said as much, querying what there was in the day's news that was relevant to me. I was promptly told I *was* the news. I had been quoted on page two of the morning edition of the *Dominion* newspaper, talking about a blond 5-year-old boy with an angelic face, who was on his way to prison. I wonder what it says about me that I had read the paper prior to receiving the call and had missed the article completely?

At the time of the call, I was working as Area Manager for Specialist Education Services (SES) in Nelson. I had begun a six-month contract with them in May 2000, but due to a decision to devolve the crown entity and place Special Education back within the Ministry of Education, made subsequent to my employment by SES, my contract had been extended until June 2001.

The quote that appeared in the *Dominion* had been taken from a speech I had given the previous evening at a Restorative Justice meeting in Wellington, a meeting I had flown up from Nelson to attend. I had been made aware before the meeting that there was a reporter present, but felt comfortable with the intended content of my speech and hadn't thought it necessary to check if and how he was going to report on what I said.

Prior to my appearance at this meeting, I had spoken publicly a number of times in the 18 months since my resignation from the position of Manager of Christchurch Women's Prison. I had never felt the need for speech notes, considering that I knew my subject matter well enough to speak off the cuff; thanks to the training in public speaking given to me by the nuns at St Mary's College in Wellington, I felt very little nervousness at the prospect of standing before an audience to speak. The title I gave to my speech, whenever it was necessary to provide one, was 'The Journey to Prison — who goes and why? What has it got to do with me?'

It certainly made a good headline — *5-year-old cited as future killer* — and the publication of the article in the paper has proven to be a defining moment for me. Sometime later, it was interesting to hear that the reporter had no sense of being the person who started the ball rolling. One of his colleagues told me of a comment he had made to her, in which he expressed his hope that his article hadn't 'contributed to' the difficulties I was experiencing. Little did he know!

In beginning this book by talking about this incident, it is not my intention to provide details regarding my contract with SES and its termination that I would not provide to the media at the time. That is no one's business but my own. Nor do I intend to re-litigate the issue of whether I did or did not identify an individual child. I am clear I was not speaking about one particular child and those who choose not to believe me are free to do so. As far as I am concerned, those issues have been dealt with, and in the overall context of the issues we as a society are now confronting, are unimportant. What we need to stay focused on is the reality that there are a number of 5-year-olds in our communities, some even younger, who are destined to come to prison, having killed or seriously injured someone along the way, unless there is a significant level of positive intervention in their lives.

How do I know this? Because I have seen them in prison visiting rooms; because every primary school principal I have met in recent times has told me the child I spoke of attends their school (some kindergarten teachers too); and, because I have been around long enough to have seen the child I first met when he was 5 years old appear at the prison gates as a young man sentenced to a term of imprisonment after he had committed a serious violent offence. It is a reality no one can deny, much as we all might want to, and no amount of burying our heads in the sand will make the reality disappear.

If I was not thinking of a specific 5-year-old child, why then did I talk about 'him' in such detail? Because I am a storyteller — that is what I do. I work to bring to life the stories of people I have met during time spent in the country's prisons, in an effort to help middle New Zealand understand that, contrary to popular belief, this is not a land of equal opportunity, nor is it a place where everyone can make it if they are willing to try. It is in the telling of their stories that those with difficult backgrounds can begin to sort out the chaos of their lives and by my telling their stories on their behalf I can also assist in that process. That is what I was doing at the meeting in Wellington and what I will continue to do as long as the opportunities to do so continue to present themselves.

The child I spoke of was blond with an angelic face for two reasons; the first, because I have met a number of blond-haired, blue-eyed, angelic-faced little boys who are at considerable risk of a life of crime and violence, given the circumstances in which they were or are living; the second, because I speak for effect, to rouse us all, myself included, out of our complacency.

It is an unfortunate fact that in my view, had I described the child as Maori, the headline would not have been as gripping, the story not as newsworthy. As one media person put it to me, 'he' was Pakeha and from Nelson, so it was inevitable the story would run. Let me be clear; I didn't want the story to run at all. I was simply seeking to lead the audience to whom I was speaking to an understanding that prison can happen to anyone and a number of youngsters in this country are on their way into prison long before they know their two-times table.

But run the story did. Within eight hours of the phone call from the *Kim Hill Show*, my contract with SES had been terminated and for the first time in my adult life, I was unemployed. Within 36 hours of that same phone call, it seemed as if I had spoken to every major media personality in the country and it had become necessary to employ a communications specialist, Glenda Hughes, to assist me with media enquiries.

As I woke on the Saturday morning, my first full day of unemployment behind me, I recall thinking that at least it was over, things would now begin to calm down and I could begin the process of making some sense of what had happened and putting my life back together. That thought proved to be a little premature. Not long after the thought passed through my mind, the phone rang and Glenda informed me I was in the *Dominion* again, this time occupying a significant portion of the front page, photo included. It would seem life was *not* going to return to anything like normal for quite some time . . . and it didn't.

I was clear from the start that I would not be involved in direct contact with the media until I had some clarity about just what had happened and why. I am a firm believer that there are no mistakes in life — what happens to us happens for a reason, but on this occasion that view had been severely challenged. I knew I would need some time and some wise counsel from close friends if I was going to be able to make any sense of it. As it turned out, it proved to be a long time before I could make any sense at all of the complete disruption of my life in Nelson that occurred.

It took me quite some time to get used to seeing images of myself walking down the wings of Christchurch Women's Prison run across the television screen and my name being spoken by various media personalities. I soon got sick of seeing the same piece of film being used over and over again and imagined others were feeling the same. I began to wish they had another piece of film to use, but was definitely not willing to provide it. While I was not enjoying being the lead story on a number of news bulletins, I did manage the occasional smile as I repeatedly heard myself described as a senior public servant.

I had never thought of myself that way, and still don't, and wondered how those whom I considered to be the real senior public servants would feel hearing that description being used about me.

I also struggled with hearing my name mentioned so frequently by politicians. On one occasion I was told by Matt Robson, whom I had met before becoming headline news, that I had been discussed in Cabinet that day. I asked if that meant I'd 'made it', to which he replied, 'No, it means you're in trouble.' On a *Face The Nation* programme on which I had declined to appear, the issue of children at risk was debated by two Cabinet ministers, a school principal and a youth worker. As I sat in my bedroom in Nelson and watched the programme, a feeling of total disconnection from reality descended. I was being discussed by five people, only three of whom I had actually met, and it seemed as if no matter where the topic led as the programme progressed, it was impossible for any of the participants to talk for more than three minutes without my name being mentioned. I was being spoken about in very positive and flattering terms and I was appreciative of that fact, but at the same time I was gaining a very strong sense of the term 'public ownership'.

The feeling of disconnection from reality is one I will remember for a long time — who was this woman they were talking about? How on earth had I provoked such a wide-ranging debate by simply naming what I knew? I am still not sure I know the answers to those questions.

The media interest blazed on for some time and I became inured to it to a certain degree. My daughter, Rebekah, was very good at keeping me, and other members of my family, up to date as each news item appeared on the Stuff.co.nz website. We made it to item number 39 before interest abated and another story claimed the media's attention. It possibly says something about what my children have had to endure as I have pursued my interest in social justice issues that when Rebekah emailed my son, Gene, in Western Australia to tell him I had a new email address as I no longer worked for SES, he described his first thoughts to me later as *I wonder what Mum's done now?*

And the rest is, as they say, history. At the conclusion of the enquiry conducted by the State Services Commission at the request of the Minister, Trevor Mallard, it was agreed that I had been treated unfairly, primarily because I had not been asked prior to my contract with SES being terminated whether I had in fact been speaking about an individual child.

To redress what was seen as unfair treatment, I was offered the opportunity to work with schools in Nelson for the remainder of the school year, an offer I was happy to accept as it gave me the chance to further investigate the reality being faced by some of the children deemed by schools to be at risk.

The work was demanding, but I enjoyed myself immensely. I met some wonderful people, including kids within whom real magic exists in spite of the very poor start in life they have been given. I was humbled by the determination to make the very best of the life they found themselves in that I saw on many of the children's faces. Perhaps best of all, I had the opportunity to gain an even deeper understanding of the degree of violence and abuse in the lives of some children in this country and was affirmed in my belief that unless we come to understand how the world looks from their perspective and are willing to help them in their quest for success, the inevitable result of the lives they are currently living is prison or death.

We have some work to do — it's time we began.

2 My journey

When the idea of writing a book was first mooted, I was clear both with myself, and with the publisher, that its primary focus was not to be my life experience. I don't consider my life interesting enough to merit an autobiography and such an idea had no appeal. What has become evident as the idea has progressed, however, is that before I move on to talk about how I think we might work together as a society to deal with some of the more challenging social issues, it might be useful if I pause to outline the life and work experience on which my particular thoughts are based. I don't consider my life experience to be any different to that of many New Zealanders, a mixture of good and bad, of success and failure — the stuff of an ordinary life. Given that it has been a fairly ordinary life to date, I often find myself wondering how it is that I am now in the process of putting my thoughts on the subject of social justice down on paper. Another question I am still not sure I know the answer to, but I shall proceed nonetheless.

I grew up in Wellington having spent the first six years of my life in Waiouru. I have two older brothers and a younger sister. My father was a returned soldier and an alcoholic. Although we were very much a middle-class family, my mother going out to work once we moved to Wellington to ensure her children had the opportunities she considered would be created by a good Catholic education, family life wasn't particularly easy for any of us, my parents included. After attending a Catholic primary school in Tawa, I spent five years at St Mary's College, in Wellington, where I learned, amongst other things, the art of public speaking, something that seems to have stood me in good stead.

I was considered a good student and even made it to prefect status in the seventh form, much to my surprise and the surprise of one or two others. I passed University Entrance in the sixth form, but due to an increasing inability to understand the world of mathematics and a resistance to learning Latin, I didn't pass my seventh form bursary exams. Nonetheless I was considered to have the necessary intelligence to pursue a university degree and so I went on to Victoria University. I had no idea what I wanted to do with my life, but all my friends were going to university, so it seemed an OK thing to be doing. With that as my prime motivation, it isn't surprising that shortly after leaving the confines of school and entering a much freer environment, I discovered there was more to life than doing what was expected. I began to enjoy the freedom and as a result, my university career on that first round was not particularly successful. Three papers and two passes the first year, three papers and only one pass the second. But I certainly managed to have some fun along the way.

I met my husband late in my first year at university — he was a friend of my brother's and, at the time I met him, was serving an apprenticeship at the railway workshops in Woburn. We became engaged in July the following year and married in January 1973. I returned to university briefly at the beginning of the new academic year, but it wasn't long before my interest in academic study waned completely and I joined the workforce full time, albeit briefly. My husband was by now a qualified diesel fitter and within two years of our marriage we were living in Twizel, where he worked on the hydroelectric project involved in building the dam at Lake Pukaki. We remained in Twizel for two and a half years before moving on to Savage River in Tasmania, the site of an iron-ore mine, and then to Bougainville, in Papua New Guinea, where he was working in a gold mine. My daughter was born in Twizel, my son in Savage River. The marriage didn't survive and I returned to New Zealand with my two children, who were by then aged five and two.

Realising I would need to complete my degree if I was to have any chance of earning enough money to raise my children well, I returned to university, part time for the first two years and full time for the final year. It wasn't an easy time. The combination of small children, work and study meant there were generally no spare hours in the day. It is a time in my life when I consider I came to truly understand the word exhaustion. But I had family help at hand with my mother living nearby, and we survived. I managed to fit my study in those first two years around a part-time job that gave us enough money to live on, but it was always a major juggling act. At the end of the second year I decided I would go on the Domestic Purposes Benefit for the next year and make a concerted effort to get the degree finished. That proved to be an experience all of its own.

It was my intention to remain on the benefit for only one year, my rationale being that once I was earning a salary, I would repay the benefit I had received several times over through my taxes. Such a positive view did little to help in dealing with the sense of failure that regularly threatened to wash over me at the idea that I had become a statistic. I was a 'solo mother', a label that was then, and is still now, thrown around with great abandon and no shortage of implied judgement by the community, the media and some of those charged with administering the benefit. The 'us and them' mentality I often find myself raging against now as various sectors of society attempt to cast judgement on those they consider to be inferior was very prevalent then. It was a salutary experience to realise I was being judged as one of 'them'. My stand against such a judgement was to insist I was a single parent, not a solo mother, a stand I continue to make today if the label drifts my way.

As it turned out, I stayed on the benefit for two years. I had a very full study programme in my final year and as it drew to a close, I noted my exhaustion levels and how little time I had spent with my children during the year. I decided we would take some time out as a family before I sought full-time work. By this time the children's father was working in Western Australia and contact with him was intermittent, so I decided to stay on the benefit and head north to Gisborne, his home town, and look for a place to live on the East Coast for a year. My purpose in making the move was threefold.

My degree was in Maori and Anthropology and having an idea by then that I would like to work in the area of social justice when I did take up full-time work, I thought time spent on the East Coast would assist more in grounding me in the reality of life for many Maori in New Zealand than the study of Te Reo and Nga Tikanga on a university campus had done, especially given my middle-class Pakeha background. I wanted to pause and enjoy some time with my children: to be home when they got home from school each day; not to be forever telling them to be quiet while I studied; to laugh with them; to know them. And I wanted my children to know their father's family, to spend time with them, to build relationships with them that would survive into adulthood. Given that it seemed likely their father would spend at least the next few years in Western Australia, I considered it important I help build a relationship between the children and his family.

As it turned out, my decision to create the opportunity for my children to know their father's family had significant positive spin-offs for me. In the process I gained a second family, a family that has proven to be a major asset and a source of great delight as I have continued my journey through life. My mother-in-law has been an extraordinary source of support to me in my role of parent and I am not sure I would have made it through the more difficult times without her; she has indeed been one of my guardian angels. I consider I am very lucky to have been given entry to her family and my life is richer because of it.

Having made the move to Gisborne, we lived with my in-laws for about a month before I found a place to live in Tokomaru Bay. In return for accommodation I worked part time as housekeeper for the Busby family, direct descendants of Sir James Busby, a significant person in the history of New Zealand. I remained living on the Coast for 10 months. It was a wonderful time, full of new experiences for a woman who had been raised in the city, and a time of stark contrasts, the memories of which remain with me today and continue to influence my view of the world.

I thought often in the course of my stay about the fact that a silver platter sat on a sideboard in the house in which I cooked and cleaned each day, a platter inscribed with a personal message from Queen Victoria to Sir James Busby, while a few kilometres away in the Tokomaru Bay community, a number of families were living in houses with dirt floors. There is no judgement intended in my observation of the contrast; rather it is something that has added to my sense of the different places in which people begin their lives. Perhaps this is where I first began to notice the difference.

As I think back to my days on the Coast, one delightful memory concerns the challenge I seemed to present to some of the local Maori in terms of my chosen lifestyle. I was in conversation with some members of a local shearing gang when I was asked where my man was. I replied that I didn't have a man, it was just my two children and I. There was a pause while that piece of news was digested and then a look of total disbelief passed across the faces of those present. As the conversation continued, it soon became evident that they thought I was kidding, and had a man hidden away somewhere I wasn't prepared to tell them about. It seemed the idea of a woman being able to live without a man just wasn't credible.

My children and I returned to Wellington at the beginning of 1984 and I obtained employment as a Probation Officer in Lower Hutt, a job I held for two years. Part of my responsibilities involved visiting offenders who had been remanded in custody prior to sentencing to allow time for a pre-sentence report to be prepared for the court. These reports outlined the sentencing options available to the judge within the context of the offender's life history and previous offending. As I continued to make regular visits to Wellington Prison and Wi Tako (now Rimutaka) Prison in Upper Hutt to interview offenders, I became increasingly conscious of the male prison environment, in particular the degree to which they remained male bastions, and became curious about the fact that many of the men who had been sentenced for crimes of violence against women were detained in these places without any apparent challenge being offered to the view they held of women.

Having completed their sentence in such a place, these men were then released back into society with the expectation that they would not offend again. My conversations with prison staff during my visits led me to believe male prisons in the mid-80s were still places where violence was the norm, both violence between inmates and violence between inmates and custodial staff.

I began to wonder how progress could be made in challenging the attitudes of offenders towards the women they had abused on their way into prison, when the world in which the state had placed them to effect their rehabilitation was full of violence, a world which seemed to accept that the more powerful you were, the more right you had to impose your will on the less powerful around you.

In a discussion held mid-1985 with a man who worked in a support role in Wellington Prison, the idea of women officers being employed in male prisons was raised and it was suggested I should apply. The discussion concerned the fact that the previous evening two officers had apparently chosen not to place an offender convicted of sex crimes against children, who had just been received at the institution, in the segregation wing, placing him instead in with mainstream inmates. The conversation between the officers that had been overheard suggested they were attempting to add their own brand of justice to the sentence imposed by the judge. Given his status as a child sex offender, the officers knew that placing him in with the mainstream inmates would expose the man to the risk of a severe beating by the other inmates. The following morning the inmate was admitted to hospital with serious injuries. The person I was speaking to believed that such events would be less likely to occur if women officers were employed in male prisons.

I will take a moment to mention at this point that male officers have always worked in female institutions, albeit until quite recently in fairly prescribed roles. They were traditionally seen as the 'heavies' with one male officer being rostered on each shift to provide support in the event of a violent confrontation with an inmate. They were not permitted to hold cell keys and were significantly more restricted in the duties they could perform and the areas they could enter than female officers were when they entered male prisons. Fortunately the value of having male officers working in female institutions today is recognised as being related more to their ability to provide the inmates with evidence that there are good men in the world than to their ability to provide back-up in a dangerous situation.

The idea of working in a male prison as an officer was at first thought totally ludicrous. Who would voluntarily walk into such an environment, I wondered? The inmates didn't concern me; I had met enough of them to dispel any sense of fear despite the nature of some of their crimes. Even then I had the sense that the majority of male inmates were boys in men's bodies, their entry into manhood having gone wrong, with entry to prison the inevitable consequence. My concerns were based more on the likely response of the male prison officers.

How would men who had worked for significant periods of time in a world that contained very few women cope with a woman coming in as one of them? How would a world predicated on power and control react when women who did not work in that way entered? The idea of applying to be a prison officer was dismissed and life as a probation officer continued.

But within a short time the idea returned. Primarily because I continued to be concerned about the degree to which the system did not challenge male inmates' attitudes to women and violence, but also for some more practical reasons. It appeared the shift work involved would mean I could see more of my children and given that I would be able to move into prison housing, it was an attractive idea from a financial perspective.

I lodged my application to be a prison officer at Wi Tako Prison about three months after the conversation at Wellington Prison and was accepted. As it turned out, I was the first woman to begin work as a custodial officer in a male prison in New Zealand, but at the time of my application, I had no idea that would be the case. The idea had been around a while and I had assumed there would be other applications in the pipeline. There was some media interest in my appointment and I can vividly recall going into a local dairy to buy the newspaper at the end of my first day to see how they had written up the story. I hoped there would be minimal fuss made as any publicity was likely to make my acceptance by male officers that much harder, as in why make a fuss of her when it's a job we've been doing for some time? As I reached for the paper that afternoon, I can remember looking down and being horrified to see my face looking back at me. They had put the story and accompanying photo on the front page. Not the best possible beginning from my perspective and I had no difficulty imagining the comments likely to come my way the next day.

I had then, and still have now, no illusions about why I was accepted for the job or why I ended up being the first woman approved to take up the role. I would like to think it was due to it becoming immediately obvious at interview that I had good communication skills and/or because it was very apparent I would add real value to the prison environment. With all due respect to those who were brave enough to appoint me, the reality as I saw it then, and still see it today, is far more pragmatic. I was 1.78 metres tall, I was no shrinking violet, I looked like I could handle myself and perhaps best of all, thanks to my experience as a probation officer, I had met a rapist and hadn't fainted. If they were going to have to take the risk of putting a woman into a male prison, and they were because pressure was building in terms of equal employment opportunity policies, it seemed I was a good first option.

New Zealand wasn't the first country to employ female officers in male prisons — we were preceded by Britain, Canada, the United States and Australia — but we were probably one of the more liberal in terms of the restrictions placed on the range of duties performed by female officers. The only thing we were not permitted to do was search inmates. In all other respects we were considered the same as our male counterparts.

There had been quite some resistance from male officers to the idea of having women work alongside them on the prison floor, but I have to say that the majority of the men I worked with were quite delightful. I suspect some acted staunch about the idea when in the company of their fellow officers, but when I was actually working with them, they were fine and in fact seemed to enjoy having some female company on the shift. Some officers had been vocal in their opposition to the idea and one or two had threatened that if a woman in uniform walked in, they would walk out. One officer in particular had been very vocal in this regard and as it happened (coincidentally or deliberately I am unsure, although I have my suspicions), he was rostered as guardroom officer on my first day. The guardroom is the hub of activities within the prison, so he was being confronted with the reality of women officers right from the word go. My sense is that he didn't enjoy that first day or any of the others I was on duty with him.

A number of officers, including the one I've just mentioned, did leave Wi Tako Prison within the first few years of the integration of female officers into male prisons. Whether their decision to resign was influenced by my arrival at the prison or by the fact women kept coming will forever be a matter of conjecture. What

I do recall is that my company seemed to be enjoyed by some male officers and tolerated by others; in contrast to the stories I was subsequently told by other women who were pioneers in other male institutions, I had a fairly easy time of it. The only time my job became a little more difficult and relationships with my male colleagues a little more tenuous was whenever media attention was focused on me. Fortunately that didn't happen very often and if I just kept my head down in the days following the appearance of an article in the newspaper, things soon returned to normal.

One area of opposition to my appointment as an officer that was a bit more of a surprise came from some of the wives of the male prison officers. The superintendent of Wi Tako Prison had found it necessary to arrange a meeting with these women once news of my appointment leaked out.

The need for the meeting was generated out of concerns being expressed by the women in a number of quarters about the increased level of risk my entry to the prison as an officer would present for their husbands. At the meeting concerns were expressed that I wouldn't be able to physically back up their husbands in the event of a violent confrontation with an inmate. Perhaps more significantly, they demanded that I not be rostered on night shift with any of their husbands. When prodded a little further by the superintendent as to the reasons for making this request, it soon became clear it wasn't a safety issue, but rather a 'temptation' issue.

There were only two officers rostered on the midnight to 8 a.m. shift and between the hours of midnight and 6 a.m. these officers were completely alone in the institution apart from the inmates, all of whom were locked in their cells. It seemed some of the wives were concerned at the idea of what their husbands might get up to if a woman was their sole companion in the early hours of the morning.

The superintendent addressed the concerns expressed about my perceived inability to back up my male colleagues in the event of a violent confrontation by talking about the fact that overseas experience had shown the presence of female officers often defused a potentially violent situation before it got out of control. In terms of their other concern, he suggested that if they had a concern about their husbands' ability to remain faithful to their marriage vows, they should take that up with their husbands, rather than expecting the Department of Justice to keep temptation out of their way. For my part, I was both flattered they saw me as a potential temptation for their husbands and concerned that the idea of men being responsible for their own behaviour was so far from the minds of these women.

As it turned out, I was rostered on to night shift within a few months of starting the job and it went well — I enjoyed the conversations I had with my colleague as we waited for dawn. Although I never quite lost my sense of envy as I left my house in the prison village around 11.15 p.m. and thought of all the people who were climbing into bed while I was beginning an eight-hour shift, I came to enjoy patrolling the institution in the dead of the night and reflecting on the lives of the men who were asleep behind the locked doors. As it happened, the officer with whom I first completed a rostered period of night shift failed to mention to his wife he was working with me and got himself into a bit of strife as a result.

One afternoon during the time we were working together, I met him and his wife in a shop in Upper Hutt. After stopping to say hello, I ended our conversation by saying I would be sure to bring the book we'd been talking about the previous night to work that evening. I noticed he gave me a rather strange look as I moved away, but it wasn't until I arrived for my shift that he told me I'd really dropped him in it with my comment and had left him with some explaining to do. Had I known, perhaps I could have assured his wife that much and all as I enjoyed her husband's company, he was actually quite safe as I was looking neither for a second husband nor a casual sexual partner.

I remained at Wi Tako Prison for almost three years. In

November 1988, I was successful in my application for a Third Officer position at Ohura Prison in the King Country, 40 minutes drive from Taumarunui, and made the move out of Wellington. A Third Officer position was the first step on the ladder of promotion as it existed at that time and at Ohura, the position involved being a shift supervisor and the person in charge of the institution after normal business hours. Ohura was at that time a small prison, from memory capable of holding only 48 inmates, and the prison at which the majority of white-collar criminals served their sentences. There were several former lawyers and one or two former police officers in residence during my time there.

I remained at Ohura for 18 months and it proved to be an interesting time for a number of reasons. The prison itself was a delight to work in. The inmates were all minimum-security and appreciative of the civilised surroundings, so were not inclined to misbehave. I was again living in the country as I had been in Tokomaru Bay and I appreciated the change of pace. And for the first time in my life, I had the opportunity to enjoy the experience of living alone. My daughter didn't wish to change schools and so had elected to stay in Wellington and board with a family friend and prior to my appointment to the position at Ohura, my son had chosen to spend his final primary school year with his father in Western Australia.

As with the time I spent in Tokomaru Bay, my time at Ohura was a great experience and has left me with both some great memories and some great ongoing friendships. I particularly enjoyed the contact I was able to have with local Maori and I used the free time I had at my disposal, given that I was temporarily a parent without children, to extend my involvement in nga mea Maori, things Maori. I taught very basic Te Reo Maori to inmates and some staff and I became involved in the prison kapa haka group.

The group was able to travel on occasion to local kapa haka competitions and enjoyed some success — nothing to do with my input. I was very much an observer from the sidelines, a silent (or perhaps not so silent) supporter.

While I was working at Ohura Prison, issues relating to the employment of female officers in male prisons had continued to surface in other male institutions around the country. By then there were female officers in all male institutions except Paremoremo, the maximum-security prison in Auckland. In that institution the male officers had voted not to work with women and their refusal to do so had gone unchallenged.

In the months following my appointment as a prison officer at Wi Tako Prison in December 1985, a woman had been employed at Rolleston Prison in Christchurch and others followed in other male institutions, but the entry of female officers into male prisons had remained a trickle rather than become a flow. By August 1986 only five women had been employed. In 1987, as a result of increasing pressure to normalise the male prison environment and ensure at least one female officer was working in each male prison, a decision was made to specifically target the recruitment of women. As a result of this campaign, 20 women were recruited and a training course designed specifically for them that paid particular attention to the issues faced by women working in the male prison environment.

The recruitment campaign and training course that was undertaken in 1987 was considered a success, but before long the difficulties being experienced by some female officers were again being discussed, both in the field and in National Office, and late in 1989, a hui of female prison officers working in male institutions was called in Wellington. I travelled from Ohura to attend. Of a total staff of 1600 prison officers, only 90 were women working in male institutions and there seemed to be a escalating number of issues emerging for these women. The Department appeared willing to concede the integration of female officers had not gone as well as it might and the hui was intended to be the place where the issues would be identified and a way forward agreed.

33

I don't think I will ever forget the introductory session at the hui. We moved our chairs into a circle and began the process of introducing ourselves and naming the institution in which we worked. Within five minutes, there were women standing to speak with tears rolling down their cheeks as they struggled to find the words to describe what it had been like to be the first female officer in their particular institution.

It was at that moment I knew that in comparison to many of my female colleagues and despite the occasional negative reaction from one or two male officers, I had enjoyed a fairly easy time of it. Some women were describing how they had worked for three years in an institution and yet were still being ignored by their male colleagues unless something work-related needed to be said. Others were describing instances of both covert and overt sexual harassment, with some of the incidents involving physical assault. The following incident gives a sense of the sort of behaviour to which some male prison officers were apparently exposing their female colleagues. This particular incident wasn't disclosed at the hui, but occurred around that time and clearly indicates the type of working environment some female officers were having to endure.

The incident involved a female officer who was standing in the control room of the institution, an area clearly visible to a number of inmates, bending down to do up her shoes. Several male officers were in the control room with her and the story goes that as she bent down to do up her shoes, one of them stepped forward, undoing the fly of his trousers at the same time as he said: 'While you're down there . . .'

I think it is indicative of the calibre of the majority of women employed in those first few years, and a credit to the particular woman concerned, that she had enough of a grip of the situation to make the immediate response: 'I don't do white boys', putting the officer behaving so appallingly back in his place. It is disturbing to think such a thing could happen in a workplace in New Zealand in the late 1980s. But in terms of the sexual and general harassment that occurred, incidents like this were just the tip of the iceberg — numerous examples were given by the women. I would like to think such incidents wouldn't happen today — or if they did, they wouldn't be tolerated and the officers looking on would find the behaviour despicable rather than humorous.

On a lighter note, one of the issues identified at the hui was the need to make a number of improvements to the uniform for female officers. Many women were unable to get uniforms in their size and were forced to wear shirts and jerseys designed for much larger male officers. There had been a blouse designed for female officers, but many were reluctant to wear it as it was made from a lightweight material that was virtually see-through — not a good look in the wings of a prison! The shirts made for male officers in a slightly heavier material were preferred, even if it meant rolling up sleeves and the shirt doubling as a slip under the uniform skirt because of its length.

There was also some dispute about the fact that the men's shirts featured pockets while the women's blouses didn't. When challenged on one occasion about this, a prison inspector known for his quick wit responded that there was no need for pockets on the women's blouses as the Department 'didn't issue bent pens'. Given our experiences of trying to get an adequate uniform, some of us weren't too sure he was joking.

A number of issues including those mentioned above were raised at the hui and then prioritized in terms of future action. The major decision made as a result of the hui was the creation of a position at National Office, which would focus on working through the issues that had been raised, as well as ensuring a better deal for both female officers and members of the other groups identified in the State Sector Act 1988. The position was titled Equal Employment Opportunity (EEO) Coordinator (Penal Division). Given the increasing anger I was feeling about the treatment being meted out to female officers working in male prisons, I didn't need much encouragement to apply. I was successful in my application and returned to Wellington to begin work in March 1990. I immediately renamed the position (in my mind) as 'official shit stirrer for women'.

It was true there were other groups whose needs required addressing in what was still a very Pakeha- and male-dominated work environment, but it was my view at the time that it would primarily be through the process of addressing the issues being raised by female officers working in male prisons that the chauvinistic attitudes prevailing at all levels in the organisation would be successfully challenged, and wedges driven into the old ways of behaving.

While it is a little off the topic of the work experience on which my particular thoughts are based, I will pause here for a moment to describe some of the patterns of behaviour within the organisation that leave me comfortable in describing the environment existing from 1985, and as late as 1990, as both chauvinistic and male-dominated.

There was an amazing rugby-based culture in the prisons. Traditionally it hadn't been necessary to advertise prison officer vacancies. Rather, the practice seemed to be to announce any vacancies at the local rugby club. If you were interested, you just had to head up to the prison for a chat. As I came to understand it, there were two main reasons things were done that way.

If you were a rugby player you were likely to have what it took to survive in the prison environment. The second and perhaps more important reason: depending on what position you played in your local rugby team, you might prove to be a major asset in the prison team as the time approached for the national prison officers' rugby tournament. According to stories I was told as I toured the country to speak to prison staff about the concept of EEO, when you headed up to the prison to check on the vacancy, the only question asked after your name was what position you played in the local rugby team. If you gave the right answer in terms of the current vacancies in the prison team, the job was yours. I was also told stories of people being approached and offered the job of prison officer because they were known to play in the position for which there was a vacancy in the prison rugby team.

On the other hand, in some prisons, such as Mt Eden Men's Prison, the criteria were even less stringent. Mt Eden was then, and still is, an awful place in terms of the physical surroundings in which staff have to work and inmates have to live. Many stories have been told of would-be officers accepting a position, picking up their uniform and turning up for work on the first day, only never to be seen again after completing their first shift, such was their shock at seeing the environment in which they were required to work. Given this difficulty in retaining staff, I was told on a number of occasions that the application process for a prison officer at Mt Eden Men's Prison had been streamlined over the years and involved one very simple test. If you could untie and re-tie the laces of your shoes, you were in.

In today's world it's hard to imagine such employment practices being acceptable within a government department, but the Prison Service had been a very closed paramilitary organisation that didn't welcome change or innovation. I believe the decision to employ female officers in male institutions was a pivotal moment in terms of beginning the necessary change. Little wonder that the women who were in the first vanguard of female officers weren't welcomed with open arms.

Having taken up the position of EEO Coordinator for the Penal Division, there appeared to be two main tasks awaiting me. I was to undertake a tour of the country to help prison staff come to terms with the reality of EEO and the likely effect of the passing of the State Sector Act on their workplace, and I was needed as a member of a working party that had been set the task of determining how best to get female officers safely into Paremoremo Maximum Security Prison.

In terms of the latter task, the then Prime Minister, Geoffrey Palmer, had stood in the House in December 1989 and declared that female officers would be working in Paremoremo by the end of the following year.

The EEO tour was quite an experience. It involved visiting 17 institutions over an 18-month period, holding 69 seminars and addressing approximately 1070 prison staff. In some institutions the prison staff boycotted the seminars and only attended when they were ordered to do so. As you can imagine, being ordered to attend a seminar featuring discussion on the subject of equal employment opportunity did little to endear me to those who had been ordered to attend, but we managed to get by. I learned to be as provocative as I needed to be to get a rise out of the person who appeared to be the most resistant to being there and once I had the bite I needed, things generally quietened down and we got on with business.

The best thing about the seminars was that once the initial resistance had been overcome, the officers themselves would often give me examples of the bruising nature of employment in the prison service, the very thing EEO policies were working to alleviate. The women who entered the male prisons as officers may have had a hard time of it, but it proved to be no worse than the experience of many of the new male recruits. Some spoke of not being spoken to by their fellow officers for their first two years; others spoke of being told by a senior officer when they asked about the duties they were supposed to perform on a certain shift: 'Fuck off and find out for yourself.' It appeared there was a tough initiation process that wasn't named and that new recruits had to find their own way through. I frequently had a male officer who had adopted a belligerent and defensive attitude in the seminar seek me out afterwards to tell me of the experiences he had endured as he settled into the job. A number of these men carried some fairly deep emotional scars as a result of their experiences.

In the course of the tour, I managed to obtain a repertoire of stories about the influence rugby had on the selection and promotion processes within the prison service. Although it was a serious issue and one that frequently tested my sense of humour, as I continued to learn about the ways in which people who didn't play or support the game had been disadvantaged in their employment opportunities, there was the occasional moment when I couldn't help laughing at the story I was being told. One such moment came at a seminar being held at Wellington Prison.

The staff at the prison were among those who had refused to attend a seminar on EEO issues and it was only when an order to attend was issued by the head of the prison service that the seminar was scheduled to proceed. I knew as I went in that I was entering staunch rugby territory. By then I had developed a reputation for badmouthing the rugby influence, and the fact they had been ordered to attend meant that as the seminar got underway, I could detect a reasonable degree of hostility among the participants. After a while, however, they began to thaw and a two-sided dialogue began.

As I talked about the undue influence I felt rugby had on the selection and promotion processes within the prison service, there were a few groans and then the staff training officer (STO) put up his hand. I had been saying that it seemed to me the second question in every job interview held to fill a prison officer vacancy was, 'What position do you play in a rugby team?' The STO agreed he had asked that question many times, but defended his right to do so, saying that the answer revealed a great deal about the applicant.

He went on to explain that a person who was a prop was obviously good at working in with others, a captain was good at getting people to work together and a halfback was quick on his feet. I asked what would happen if I turned up for an interview and said I didn't play rugby. Unfazed, he replied that he would then ask what sport I did play, in response to which I asked: 'What if I said I didn't play any sport?' There was a brief pause and then with a grin, the STO looked me straight in the eye and said: 'Well, then I'd know I definitely should employ you — you could cover the roster while every other bastard was away playing rugby.'

Getting female officers into Paremoremo Prison also involved seminars; seven of them, each one attended by approximately 30 prison staff, with the title 'Women officers are coming to Paremoremo. What can we do to make it easier on them and you?' The good thing was that on this occasion, I wasn't conducting the seminars on my own. Several other members of the Working Group also took part. As with the EEO seminars, staff had been ordered to attend these seminars and consequently there was considerable resistance to hearing the information being shared. This was late 1990 and the officers had held out against having female officers in the institution for five years. They weren't pleased to think the system was finally moving against them. The Working Group had determined that the first female officers to work at Paremoremo would be women who had worked in other male institutions. This was seen as one way of reducing the level of risk as the staff and inmates got used to the idea of having women working there.

For my part, I can clearly recall the seminars and the degree of fear displayed by the officers (manifesting predominantly as belligerence) as they faced the reality they would soon have to work with women.

Within the first 10 minutes at each of the seven seminars, someone in the audience would put up their hand and say: 'You can't bring women in here to work, my wife won't like it.' It seemed as if we were back at the meeting held five years earlier by the superintendent of Wi Tako, with the wives of some of his officers. As he had done on that occasion, we reminded those officers concerned about the reaction of their wives to the idea female officers were coming to work in the institution that it wasn't the role of the Department to consider the views of spouses in determining policy. Nor was the Department responsible for the state of the officers' marriages.

The other issue raised at every seminar concerned what the

male officers seemed to see as the inevitability of them being required to have regular sex with the female officers. Some even managed to convey the sense that it would be a chore they would be reluctant to undertake. I can remember quite vividly having to remind the male members of the audience in reasonably blunt terms on more than one occasion that they were not obliged to share what they had between their legs with every woman they met. Nor, in fact, did every woman want it. It was definitely not the sort of dialogue that usually occurred between National Office and field staff, but it seemed at the time as if only very blunt speaking would get the message across.

Female officers didn't enter Paremoremo Maximum-Security Prison by the end of 1990 as Geoffrey Palmer had predicted, but three female officers did begin work there in March 1991 and as had been the case in all other prisons, they very quickly came to terms with the new environment and demonstrated a strong aptitude for the job.

I moved out of the position of EEO Coordinator in August 1993. I then worked for 12 months in a role that involved assisting at a management level with change that was being introduced into the prison service before being offered a secondment to the position of prison inspector, a role I accepted and held for 15 months.

The role of prison inspector involves oversight of the safe and humane containment of inmates, oversight that takes the form of institution visits during which an interview is held with any inmate who has requested to be seen.

It also involved conducting special investigations following the occurrence of any incident within an institution deemed to be serious, for example an assault on an officer or a death in custody.

I agreed to accept the secondment into the role of prison inspector because I felt it would put me back in touch with inmates and inmate issues. It seemed in a way as if I had come full circle and my attention could return to the issues that had taken my interest when I had first become a probation officer: the degree to which prison is, or can be, used as a place to confront offenders with the chaos of their lives and empower them to make real changes; the attitudes held by many male offenders towards women, attitudes that often lay at the heart of the reasons they were in prison; and the journeys offenders have taken as they have made their way into prison.

Although I was returning to where I had started, I was soon to have the opportunity to look at the issues from a new perspective. It was as a prison inspector that I had my first real contact with women in prison and began to see the connectedness of the journeys that were being taken to prison. Some of the women I met had raised sons who were now in prison while others were the wives or partners of the men I had met during my time on the floor at Wi Tako and Ohura Prisons. It was at this point I began to realise that a strong woman was often at the centre of many of the families who were rotating through the criminal justice system and that it might well be through these women that real change could be effected within these same families.

In taking up the role of prison inspector, I also found a new cause to champion. My role wasn't restricted to inspecting female prisons, in fact I can recall visiting every one of the 17 prisons in the country during my time as inspector, but I did begin to focus a little more on the management of women in prison. In doing so, I began to notice the degree to which they were the poor cousins of the men in prison. They were allocated fewer resources than the men and there was almost no recognition of the differences between men and women in prison, differences that were easily discernable if time was taken to notice them. I could see the system was being driven by the needs of men in prison and prison policies were being written with men in mind. The women in prison were expected to be grateful for what they did receive and to comply without complaint to the male-focused policies. I had found a new cause.

In January 1996 the opportunity arose to take up a position at Christchurch Women's Prison and I accepted. My journey to what I had begun to consider the heart of the issue was underway.

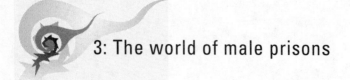

3: The world of male prisons

My first day as a female custodial officer in a male prison in many ways encapsulates the sense I have retained of male prisons as 'overgrown' boarding schools — places filled with boys occupying men's bodies. They are places where many young men go simply as part of the process of becoming adults, where testosterone bounces off the walls and big kids take a break from the real world.

As I begin my description of life within male prisons as I experienced it, I need to make the point that my sense of them being places filled with boys occupying men's bodies is in no way intended to make light of the inmates' offences, or to excuse them from culpability. Many of them have committed vicious crimes and have brought enormous grief to the lives of their victims and their victims' families. However, as I became more familiar with the environment, I became increasingly conscious of the underlying immaturity of many of the male inmates and the degree to which their emotional development appeared to have been impaired by the circumstances of their upbringing. It was this that led to my sense of many of them being big kids who were taking a break, an imposed break, from the world.

In December 1985, male prisons were still very much paramilitary institutions. The management structure of each male prison at that time included a superintendent, a First Officer (known fondly as the Chief or 'God') and various Second and Third Officers. At Wi Tako (now Rimutaka) Prison, every weekday morning at 8 a.m. a staff parade was held at which the relevant news of the day was distributed to staff and any messages (or warnings) the superintendent or the Chief wanted to impart were passed on. It was a reasonably formal occasion with staff uniforms being inspected as part of the process. It was a big day when someone — me — turned up in uniform, but wearing a skirt rather than trousers.

Just prior to the staff parade each morning, inmates were required to gather in the prison compound and line up in their various work gangs. They were allowed to continue to talk among themselves and smoke until the staff parade had finished and the door leading to the compound was opened, signalling the 'brass' were on their way out. As the door opened, the officer overseeing the inmate parade would call 'smokes out' and the inmates were expected to extinguish their cigarettes, stop talking and (on a good day) stand up straight and look enthusiastic about the fact they were about to begin a day's work.

When the staff arrived on the inmate parade ground, the Chief would announce anything it was considered the inmates needed to know about changes to prison rules or routines before the inmates were inspected by the officers in charge of the various work parties for the day. The inspection was to ensure the inmates had the right clothing and equipment for the work they were about to undertake. They would then be dismissed from the parade and move off to their various work sites.

The morning I began work as a prison officer, the inmates very quickly became aware something was up. They knew a woman officer was scheduled to start work — it had been reported in the media the previous week — and they were on the alert thinking it likely I would be on the parade that morning.

Although the door through which the management team entered the prison compound was some distance from the inmate parade ground, they could see as soon as the group emerged that someone wearing a skirt was walking beside the superintendent. As I drew closer, some inmates recognised me (I had,

45

after all, been the probation officer for a number of them during the previous two years — perhaps not a very effective probation officer, given they were in prison!) and before long many of them were calling out my name.

The compound began to resound to shouts of: 'Hey Ces, how ya doing?' 'Way to go, Ces.' I was unwilling to look at the face of either the superintendent or the Chief. The formal occasion had been completely undone, chaos appeared to be on its way and I could see nearly every male officer present thinking: 'See, told you — a woman's been here five minutes and the decay's already setting in.' From my perspective, it was definitely not the best possible start.

The day eventually got underway. I was attached to an officer for the eight-hour shift and it was intended that I spend the day simply following him around to get a sense of the physical lay-out of the prison, the daily routines and of the inmates themselves. After my somewhat inauspicious start, I can recall being determined to try to stay quiet and out of trouble for the rest of the day and I think I actually managed it, for the first day at least. I was told sometime later that the inmates had been keen to initiate me into the prison by dousing me with water from one of the fire hoses, but due to my diligence in sticking to the side of my prison officer guide, that didn't prove possible. There was, however, one rather delightful incident on the first day, an incident that in many ways set the scene for the time I would work as a prison officer in a male prison.

The officer I was accompanying on his duties was required to do a muster, a muster being a tour of the prison grounds during which the officer matches the faces of inmates to the inmate names listed on a muster board. Musters are required every hour during the general unlock hours of a prison, the purpose being to ensure inmates are where they are supposed to be and doing what they are supposed to be doing. As part of this particular muster, the officer, with me trailing behind, entered the prison kitchen and having noted the inmates who were at work there, he indicated to me to wait while he checked the bakehouse at the rear of the kitchen. As I stood looking around, I noted a small group of inmates standing a few metres away appeared to be up to something. As I focused more directly on what was occurring, I noticed one had dropped his trousers and was in the process of pulling them back up.

He had his back to me as he did it and I quickly realised his actions were based on a desire to be the first one to acknowledge the arrival of the new female officer in an 'appropriate' way, while at the same time minimising any risk I would actually see something and embarrass him.

The inmate was totally absorbed in what he was doing and remained unaware I had spotted what was going on. The other inmates in the group had noticed, however, and were waiting to see how I would react. I was finding the situation very funny and wasn't at all concerned or affronted, so I simply sidled over and whispered close to the inmate's left ear: 'You did it too fast; you'll need to do it a bit slower next time so I don't miss anything.' It was pure delight to stand and watch the colour creep up the inmate's neck and across his face, which it did in fine style. While he was a little embarrassed at being caught out, he was also able to find the humour in the situation and laughed while waiting for the colour in his face to subside.

I was told later it was at this point the inmates knew having female officers in male prisons was going to work, the important thing apparently being that I had proven I had a sense of humour. As it turned out, I was to have endless opportunities to test my sense of humour further as I continued to oversee the management of men who had found their way to prison. There were difficult and dangerous times and I don't wish to minimise the fact that these men were in prison because they had committed a crime, often a particularly nasty crime, but the reality for me was that I spent the majority of my time as a prison officer in a male prison laughing at the antics of the inmates, as they sought to make the best of the situation in which they found themselves.

The other strong memory I have of my first day concerns the smell. In subsequent weeks I was to become used to the smell of unwashed male bodies and dirty socks — the 'stuff' of male prisons — but on my first day, that wasn't the case. As I walked the wings for the first time, the institution literally reeked of aftershave. I began to wonder if this was the norm, but the more experienced officers quickly assured me that wasn't the case, obviously as surprised as I was at the way many of the inmates had chosen to acknowledge my arrival. My fellow officers were adamant they'd never smelt as much aftershave in the wings as they did that day and suggested I enjoy it as it was unlikely to last, aftershave costing what it did. They were right, it didn't last and I soon became accustomed to the smells more usually associated with large groups of men living together.

As I settled into the job, the inmates and I found a way of getting along together. For the most part they were respectful in their treatment of me and responded well to the management technique of 'firm but fair'. There were some who struggled with the idea that a woman could tell them what to do and I worked hard to ensure I wasn't overly confrontational in my dealings with those particular men. The inmates generally seemed to understand they were in prison and certain rules and regulations applied. For the most part it seemed they just wanted to get through each day without incident and regularly showed they enjoyed the opportunity to gain a woman's perspective on an issue or some aspect of their life. For my part, I enjoyed the chance to challenge their view of women, to increase their awareness of our humanity, the fact that women are not just something to own and abuse. For some inmates, quite a number in fact, it appeared this was the first time in their lives they had been confronted with the idea of women as people rather than as sex objects or punching bags.

I vividly recall a conversation held one day as I supervised a work party in the grounds surrounding the prison. The inmates were discussing the behaviour of women in general and some of the women they knew in particular. The conversation had been underway for some time before I tuned into it, my mind bringing it into total focus as I heard one inmate say that when a woman walked into a bar wearing a short skirt, she definitely wanted 'it', regardless of what she might say. I joined in the conversation at this point and expressed the view that it didn't matter what a woman was wearing — if she was asked and the answer she gave was no, she meant no. The ensuing conversation was both humorous and concerning.

The inmates all agreed women always said no when they meant yes. It was part of the male/female game as they saw it, and all were confident in their view that every woman wanted 'it', particularly when the women had the opportunity of getting it from these virile young men. As they continued to work and I continued to supervise, I attempted to explain that even if a woman was standing in front of them stark naked and they asked her if she wanted to have sex with them, if she was shaking her head and saying no, they should consider that she meant exactly that — no. For some of the inmates in the work party, this was definitely a new and somewhat novel idea.

One source of endless humour with the inmates was the process involved in doing muster checks in the bathrooms of the prison wings. It was always going to be necessary for me to check those areas as part of any muster because if the inmates knew they were no-go areas for me, the bathrooms would immediately become the areas in which to use any drugs they managed to smuggle into the institution and conduct any other 'business'.

Given this fact, prison management decided the best way to protect the modesty of the inmates was to put up shower curtains, the idea being that I would call out as I entered the area and any inmate present would then be able to walk over to the curtain and pull it back far enough to let me see him, while protecting his sense of modesty. It was a good idea, but unfortunately it wasn't quite in line with what the inmates had decided.

The curtains went up and within hours the inmates had cut

a series of holes in them at groin level. This meant I got a very well-framed view of a certain part of the anatomy of any inmate taking a shower every time I entered a prison bathroom during my first few days as a prison officer. The vandalised shower curtains came down, new ones went up, but within hours the same thing happened again. As the prison budget obviously wasn't going to run to providing a new set of shower curtains every few days, and given that the inmates didn't appear too alarmed at the idea I might see them naked, the decision was made to remove the second set of curtains and let nature take its course, as it were. I then developed my own idea, suggesting to the inmates that I would call out as I walked into the bathroom areas, thus allowing any inmate taking a shower a few seconds to turn to face the wall, while turning their face back towards me. It seemed to me this practice would allow the preservation of at least a little modesty.

The inmates accepted my suggestion, but in its application modified it just a little. Within days the new procedure was firmly established.

Each time I was preparing to enter a bathroom area and called a warning, every inmate taking a shower would ensure they were facing me with their backs to the wall as I entered. They would stand like a line of soldiers on a parade ground and wait patiently with grins on their faces while I marked their names off on the muster board. The inmates were confident I would eventually break under the pressure and give in to the temptation to look lower than their faces and each time I entered a bathroom, they persuaded themselves this was going to be the time. I am pleased to be able to report that I never did weaken and lower my eyes, but rather than that being because I have iron willpower, it was because I had no need at all to drop my gaze — they never realised I had great peripheral vision.

In many ways the issue of how I handled male nudity was the rite of passage for my acceptance as a female officer in a male prison environment. I survived the first test by finding humour in the inmate dropping his trousers for me on my first day of duty and it seemed the second test was contained within my reaction to the vandalising of the shower curtains and the subsequent need to enter the bathrooms unsure of quite what I would find.

There were various smaller tests along the way, with inmates regularly suggesting they had exactly what I needed to make my life truly complete if I wished to avail myself of it (they made it abundantly clear they weren't talking about wealth and status, but something a little more basic). As long as I responded with humour and was careful not to completely emasculate them in my reply, it seemed as if the situation was manageable. While my self-esteem wasn't dependent on the men with whom I interacted in the wings of the prison finding me sexually attractive, nonetheless I was careful to acknowledge the compliment implied in their suggestions. I felt it was useful they saw me as a sexual being while at the same time having to process the reality that I was a person in my own right — someone who experienced thoughts and feelings in the same way they did.

What was to prove the final test of acceptance in this regard came unexpectedly a few months into the job, and involved an inmate serving a term of life imprisonment for murder. The 'lifers' hadn't been too welcoming when I first entered the institution. These were the men who were at the top of the prison inmate hierarchy. They had a long time to serve and tended to keep to themselves, letting the day-to-day activities of the younger, more boisterous inmates pass over their heads. They generally only became involved in events within the prison wings if the conditions in which they were serving their sentence were at stake.

For the first few months of my time at Wi Tako, the lifers had tended to ignore me, possibly seeing the introduction of female officers into male institutions as a passing phase.

On this particular day, I was standing at the end of a prison wing when a lifer emerged from the bathroom area at the other end of the wing. He'd obviously just had a shower and was naked, his only piece of attire a towel thrown over his shoulder.

There was a reasonable distance between us, but as he walked towards me, he began a conversation. I quickly realised this was some sort of test, so I entered into the conversation and held his gaze as he walked towards me. We chatted for what seemed an eternity but must have been only minutes, with me taking care to ensure my eyes never strayed from his as he continued to make his way up the wing to his cell, which was to the immediate right of where I was standing. Reaching his cell door, he entered the cell and pushed the door shut, only to open it a few seconds later and wink at me while saying: 'Not bad, Miss.' It would seem I had passed the test.

With regard to the difficult times, in four and a half years of working on the floor of male prisons, I was threatened and in fear of my physical safety only once and that was as a direct result of my own inappropriate behaviour.

I was tired due to the fact I had only an eight-hour break between shifts (entirely my choice), I didn't like this particular inmate and in an early morning exchange with him, I swore at him, telling him to go away in less than polite terms. I turned back to the task at hand and didn't concern myself with what he was doing. He moved away from me, but returned only minutes later with a scythe on his shoulder, obviously determined to finish the conversation I hadn't wanted to have with him. I stood for several seconds rubbing the top of my arm as I anticipated the arc the scythe would follow when he swung it, while I considered how to get out of the situation into which I had put myself.

The situation resolved itself without violence, I'm pleased to say, the resolution simply involving me lowering my eyes to indicate I was well aware he now had the upper hand in the conversation. After I lowered my eyes, the inmate began to back away from me, at the same time verbalising his anger. Eventually he put the scythe down. I learned a lot in that moment about the ease with which violence can be provoked in the prison environment. I also learned about the need for custodial staff to continually monitor their own behaviour in terms of the degree to which that behaviour may provoke a violent response from the inmates, people who are significantly less equipped than prison officers to manage their emotions.

The inmate was subsequently charged with threatening an officer and punished, receiving five days' solitary confinement. I was never really forced to acknowledge the incident had been of my own making, although I have since acknowledged it a number of times and am happy to do so again now. My biggest challenge at the time was persuading the other inmates not to 'deal' to the man once he was released from solitary confinement. They appeared very concerned that one of their own had threatened the wellbeing of the new female 'screw' and indicated that should I wish them to do so, they were more than willing to dispense their own particular brand of justice.

As I reflect on the time spent working on the floor of a male prison, some other delightful incidents come to mind.

It was a cold winter's afternoon, and after completing their work for the day, a group of inmates decided to play a game of touch while waiting for tea. A game of touch in the prison compound was always a fairly rough experience given that it was being played on concrete rather than grass and the inmates always appeared to be a little unclear about the difference between touch and tackle. The potential for someone to get hurt playing the game was acknowledged, but it was considered preferable to fights occurring in the prison wings as a way of inmates letting off steam. The only rule imposed by the prison was that inmates were to wear their own clothing rather than risking prison clothing being damaged.

On this particular cold winter's afternoon, I was rostered on the afternoon shift in the guardroom and had oversight of the prison compound. The game of touch got underway and I soon noticed one inmate was playing in prison gear. I picked up the microphone of the prison PA system and after saying the inmate's name, I said, 'Get the prison gear off.' The inmate concerned continued playing and after a few minutes, I again picked up the microphone and repeated my instruction. There was a slight pause in the game during which time the inmate moved to the side of the area on which the game was being played and began to strip. As he took each article of clothing off, he paused to fold it neatly before placing it on the ground and moving to remove the next one. Once completely naked, he turned to face the guardroom and bowed. To the sound of re-sounding applause from the other inmates and some officers, he then bent to pick up his clothing and moved in a very dignified fashion towards the prison wing in which he resided. As he made his way inside, I used the PA system to thank him for obeying my instruction.

Morning unlock was another interesting 'first'. The practice was that on each weekday morning, general unlock occurred at 6.30 a.m., the only inmates unlocked before then being the kitchen workers responsible for breakfast, who were unlocked an hour earlier. Two officers would do the unlock in each wing, each officer moving down one side of the wing, unlocking cell doors as they went. As I observed the general unlock for the first time, I was fascinated to see the procedure was undertaken in complete silence, the only sounds were the turn of the keys in the locks and the officers' footsteps. I had been raised in a house where it was normal practice to say 'good morning' at the start of the day to those you were living with, and found the silence both unusual and a little disconcerting. When it was my turn to do the unlock, I moved down the wing and as I unlocked each cell door, I said a cheerful 'good morning' before moving on. Nothing was said on the first day, but in the course of the unlock the following morning, as I unlocked the third cell door, a voice was very clearly heard saying, 'Fuck, she's on again.'

All of the incidents I have recounted occurred at Wi Tako Prison, where I worked as a prison officer for three years, but there were also some memorable times at Ohura Prison in the King Country. The nature of the prison and the nature of the offences that had led the Ohura inmates to prison were both quite different to my experience at Wi Tako and both increased my understanding of the different journeys taken by people to prison in this country.

The image portrayed by the media of prison inmates often leaves the impression that crime in New Zealand is a lower socioeconomic phenomenon that victimises the middle and upper classes. My time at Ohura Prison reinforced the sense I had developed, while working as a probation officer, of the reality being something quite different. There I met many white-collar criminals, including former lawyers and members of the police, men who had in some instances coldly and calculatingly committed crimes that had financially ruined the lives of their victims. It was quite noticeable from the outset that these men managed the prison system far better than their less educated fellow inmates and as a result did their time in prison a lot easier. Their comfort with the written word, their ability to read and understand prison regulations meant they were able to ensure they received all they were entitled to and were not in any way victimised by the system. Many inmates are quite passive in their acceptance of the treatment they receive in prison, but the white-collar criminals were far more proactive in that regard.

While working at Ohura, I came to realise that while it may be true that all those sentenced to a term of imprisonment in New Zealand serve their term in reasonably similar conditions, education and money can and do make a difference in a hundred ways, both in how the inmate manages the sentence and the impact of the imposition of a term of imprisonment on their lives.

The issue is not whether one type of crime is any worse than another, for example whether financial ruin has a greater impact on a victim than a home invasion. Rather, the issue is the need to acknowledge the fact that money and education are resources available to only some of the people who are drawn into the criminal justice system. As I served my time at Ohura Prison, I watched a number of well-educated men complete a term of imprisonment imposed after they had been convicted for major fraud, all the time congratulating themselves that they weren't like the 'others', the burglars and those in prison for violent offences. They appeared to be completely untouched by any sense of guilt about what they had done. In their minds it was business, business the like of which goes on every day in New Zealand, the only problem on this occasion being that their expensive lawyer hadn't found the loophole in the law that would have seen them escape conviction.

The reality that was reinforced for me at Ohura and that most New Zealanders are rarely required to confront as the merits of imposing longer and tougher sentences are debated, is that the justice system isn't always about right or wrong, although I agree it should be. It is sometimes about money and power and more often than it should be, it is also about the skin colour of the alleged offender. The disproportionately high percentage of young Maori men in prison in New Zealand cannot be ignored. Neither can it be explained away as simply the result of bad behaviour. I had been aware for some time of the issues that seemed to sit below the surface for the many disenchanted young Maori men I met in prison and some of my experiences at Ohura increased my understanding in that regard.

The most vivid example I can recall of the positive outcome able to be achieved when someone learns to value who they are and where they have come from, was a young man serving a term of imprisonment for dangerous driving causing death. He was a good-looking young Maori from the Bay of Plenty, but when I first encountered him at Ohura, he walked with his head down and was obviously lacking in self-esteem. In time it became apparent he had a real interest in learning Te Reo and kapa haka and eventually he joined the prison kapa haka group and began attending the Te Reo classes being held in the institution.

He proved to have a quick mind and an engaging personality and before long he was fully immersed in learning the Maori language and was the designated leader of the kapa haka group.

In the time I knew him, his body language changed completely. As he grew more confident in his culture, his shoulders straightened and he literally began to look the world in the eye. He led the kapa haka group to victory in a local competition, his influence as leader playing a major role in the group's success. As the time approached when he would be released from prison, he was given home leave, a parole from the prison for 72 hours. When he returned, he told me he had sought out his grandfather and had asked him to tell him his whakapapa, the genealogy of his family, something he'd had no interest in prior to coming to prison.

As a result of the conversations he had with his grandfather over that weekend, he was clear that he would never return to prison. He said that having learned about those who had gone before him, his ancestors were now sitting on his shoulders and he had their honour to uphold. That was the moment when I learned how simple it can be — connect the disenfranchised young man to the culture and history from which he comes, give him a sense of his place in the world, and he will do the rest himself.

The pranks I had been subject to at Wi Tako Prison didn't occur at Ohura Prison, possibly because by then I was a ranking officer and shift supervisor rather than an officer on the floor and the inmates didn't have the same opportunities to determine the scope of my sense of humour. I did, however, finish my time as a prison officer as I had started it, with the inmates having their fun. My last shift at the prison was a 2–10 p.m. supervision shift. As part of my duties, I was required to do a patrol of the institution and grounds before the inmates were locked in for the night. As I began this final patrol, I stepped out of the main building to find a group of inmates waiting with a bucket of water. I beat a hasty retreat but not before the back of my skirt was soaked.

I mistakenly thought that would be their only attempt at a

prank, so I waited a few minutes and then resumed the patrol, exiting the institution via another door. The patrol went smoothly until the moment when I began making my way back from the institution gardens. I sensed some movement behind one of the fences and made a mental note to avoid going in that direction. I was so busy focusing on the place where I suspected a group of inmates were waiting to continue the dousing process that I failed to notice the inmates were in fact waiting in a tree I was about to walk underneath, until it was too late.

At the same time as I realised the trap had been set, the inmates dropped down beside me out of the tree and emptied the buckets of water they were carrying all over me.

During my time at both Wi Tako and Ohura Prisons, I had become increasingly aware that while many of the inmates I was working with were responsible for serious crimes, when time was spent with them in circumstances where they didn't have access to any mind-altering substances, they appeared to be kids who had walked into trouble unwittingly and hadn't known how to get out of it. Let me be clear that I didn't see this then, nor do I see it now, as an excuse for the behaviour that had brought these men to prison and I was comfortable that prison was the place where, if all went as it should, they would finally begin to learn about action and consequence. But it was evident that the majority of those I met were not inherently bad; they were just not good at knowing when enough was enough in terms of their alcohol and drug use.

It seemed to me as I continued to focus on the journeys of the men in prison that it was primarily violent and inappropriate behaviour following excessive use of alcohol and drugs that was leading so many young men into our prisons; that and an absence of any other way to prove they were men. I don't want to give the impression that I met no evil people in prison or that I believe everyone finds their way into prison through a series of unfortunate circumstances over which they have no control. I have confronted evil on more than one occasion and have looked into the eyes of some inmates and known their soul was long gone. But if we are ever going to be successful in our quest to find a real and workable solution to the high imprisonment rate in this country, we must remain forever mindful that those who can be considered evil are the minority. They must not be the ones who drive our social justice policies.

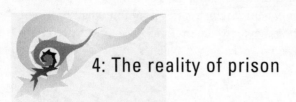

4: The reality of prison

In the previous chapter I have described a number of the incidents that occurred during my time as a prison officer in a male prison, pranks undertaken with glee by the inmates and reminiscent of the sort of pranks you might expect to occur in a boys' boarding school. As I think about the stories I have told, I am conscious that the description of my experiences as the male prison system came to terms with the entry of female prison officers could lead to the conclusion that prison is fun, too much fun, in fact. While preparing to write this book, I reviewed some audiotapes of media interviews I did in my first few years as a prison officer in which I discussed various aspects of the integration of female officers into male prisons. I noticed that whenever I was challenged about why I would want to work in the negative environment of a prison, I invariably responded because it was fun, because the characters I met in prison made me laugh. And it was, and they did. There is, however, another side to the reality of prison that leaves me in no doubt the pranks and humour I was part of were simply an attempt to make the best of a bad situation.

It is the other side of the reality of prison I want to talk about now. It is a reality that goes beyond the superficial impressions and outlines the day-to-day drudgery of life within a prison and the extent to which an inmate's personal space is constantly invaded in order to maintain the security of the institution. For some of you reading this book, this will be unwanted or unnecessary information, given that you believe it is entirely through their own actions that offenders arrive at the prison gates. I am asking you to bear with me as I describe the reality of prison, because I believe it will only be through understanding that reality that we will begin to find the answers to the ever-increasing levels of violence within our communities.

A view often expressed by members of the general public and reinforced by the media is that prisons are too soft. They see prisons as holiday camps offering three meals a day and a soft bed to those who don't wish to work, participate in any meaningful way in life or be responsible for themselves. Many see this as the reason behind our increasing prison population, and the reason why many of those who have served a term of imprisonment choose to re-offend and return. It's a comfortable idea, reinforcing the sense that entry to prison is a choice and not therefore something for which we as a society bear any responsibility. It's also an idea that seems to lead people to believe that if we can just find the appropriate blend of cruelty and encouragement in our management of them, those who find their way to prison will realise the error of their ways and make different choices in the future.

So, what is the reality of prison beyond the boyish pranks?

In 1997 and again in 1999, a theatre production was undertaken at Christchurch Women's Prison as part of the biannual Christchurch Arts Festival. The prison joined with the Festival, under the guidance of director Briony Ellis, and with the Maori drama group Te Rakau Hua o te Wao Tapu, led by Jim Moriarty, to bring to life the stories of some of the inmates, using music, dance and drama.

The experience was pure magic for all involved and impacted in a number of ways on the inmates and on the community, but at this point I want to focus on the way in which it allowed, or perhaps even forced, the public to experience a little of the reality of prison.

In the interests of both maintaining the security of the

institution and giving those coming to the performances the chance to experience a little of the reality of prison, the following steps were taken as the public entered the institution. They were asked to leave their handbags and other personal possessions in their cars, which they had to leave parked outside the prison fence; as they entered the prison building itself, they were subject to searches similar to those now commonplace at major airports, having to walk through a metal detector and on some evenings stand while a prison drug dog sniffed around them; and they were made to wait in a prison corridor (often, given the time of year, a very cold prison corridor) with the doors at either end locked until we were ready to admit them to the area where the production was being staged. This latter step was necessary because the performance began with a karanga and the audience being called into the theatre space by the performers. It also enabled us to give the audience a sense of the powerlessness involved in being a prison inmate before they experienced the show.

During the staging of the 1997 show, I spent some time each evening at the front gate, assisting staff as they undertook the somewhat daunting process of admitting 300 members of the public into the prison, while at the same time trying to maintain an appropriate level of security. It is a prison manager's nightmare in terms of the level of risk involved in allowing such large groups into a prison, but we had thought long and hard about it. We were convinced the risk was worth it, given the opportunity it presented to allow us to confront the public's perception of prison and prison inmates.

During the time I spent at the front gate before each performance, I was confronted a number of times by a member of the public demanding that they be allowed to take their handbag or personal possessions into the institution with them. These people were clearly disconcerted at having restrictions placed on their behaviour. They had read the prominently displayed signs and had taken the handouts explaining the rules relating to the maintenance of security they were offered as they handed in their tickets, but they obviously felt the rules were not intended for them. Prior to coming to talk to me, they had challenged the officer who had noticed they still had their handbag or cellphone in their possession. When they got no joy there, they then asked whom else they could speak to and were sent my way.

One woman in particular comes to mind. She had argued for some minutes with an officer about her right to take her handbag into the prison and in desperation the officer directed her to me. I outlined the reasons behind the request that the public leave all personal possessions in their cars, but she still wasn't happy and with her outrage at having to surrender her handbag very apparent, demanded to see someone 'higher'. I calmly assured her there was no one higher, I was it, and told her she had a choice to make; either she put her handbag in the boot of her car and entered the prison to see the performance (repeating yet again that the vehicle area would be patrolled throughout the duration of the performance), or she kept her handbag in her possession and went home.

I couldn't resist adding that if she paused for a moment to think about it, she would realise the handbag was likely to be a lot safer in her car — she was entering a prison after all, and a number of those inside had proven themselves very adept at acquiring other people's property! After a few minutes, somewhat reluctantly and with an extremely aggrieved look on her face, she chose to put her handbag in her car and enter the prison grounds.

A number of those coming to the performance were also upset at not being able to walk straight into the theatre space and reserve a 'good' seat for themselves and their friends. It was obvious from the tickets that there were no allocated seats, and a number of people had deliberately come early knowing the show they were attending had been sold out and hoping to be able to pick the best position from which to view the performance. As they stood in the corridor waiting to be allowed to enter the theatre space, they often became totally confused about the direction in which they would move once they were permitted to do so and made the wrong decision and pushed forward to the wrong door.

On some evenings as I made my way to the front of the crowd to indicate to the performers that the audience had gathered and we could begin, several people challenged me about the fact they had been kept waiting and expressed their disappointment at not being able to pick their own seat. These people were clearly used to having their wishes complied with and had strong expectations about their right to have their needs and wants met.

We didn't treat them in the way we did just for the fun of it; the steps we took were necessary if we were to maintain an appropriate level of security and if we were to enable the performance to start with maximum impact. However, a positive spin-off was that it also enabled us to give the audience a sense of the powerlessness involved in being a prison inmate before they became involved in the show. Many were not very keen on the experience.

I have no wish to criticise those people who struggled in the ways outlined as they entered a prison for the first time; on the contrary, I admire their courage in subjecting themselves to a new experience in an attempt to understand the world of prisons a little more. It does, however, provide food for thought for us all when attention is paid to the processes and procedures inmates are subject to as they are admitted into prison and as the daily routines needed to maintain institution security grind on.

Any inmate being received at an institution is strip-searched as a matter of course during the reception process. As I write that, I acknowledge that the word 'strip-searched' can slip somewhat easily off the tongue and many reading this will consider that is exactly as it should be, strip-searching a necessary and justified procedure within the confines of a prison. But let's pause for a moment and for those of us, myself included, who are used to enjoying enough control over our lives that we only take our clothes off in front of another person when we want to, let's imagine the reality of a strip-search. It involves stripping in front of two complete strangers in a situation where those strangers have complete power over us as evidenced by their uniform, the keys they are wearing on their belt and the fact that several of their colleagues can be called into the room within minutes should they consider that necessary, i.e., should you resist.

It is true that if a strip-search is done according to correct procedure, the inmate will never be totally naked in front of the officers doing the search. The inmate will be required to take off all the clothing they are wearing on the top half of their body and will then have the opportunity to put a T-shirt or jersey back on before being required to take off all the clothing they are wearing on their bottom half.

They will be required to run their fingers through their hair while the officers watch, to open their mouths and to expose the soles of their feet for inspection, and a female inmate may be required to lift her breasts to demonstrate nothing is being concealed beneath them.

One protection put in place for the inmate is that no officer of the opposite gender can perform a search or is permitted to be in the presence of an inmate being searched. Despite this, the situation remains a difficult one, usually uncomfortable for both the inmate and the officers. It is a demeaning process for all involved, particularly for the inmate being searched, and the bravado they may and often do display during the process is, in my view, simply a way of surviving the event.

Inmates have to endure strip-searches not just once, but many times during their time in prison. A strip-search is undertaken as the inmate is received into the institution, but that is only one of the occasions on which it is considered a necessary part of the prison routine. Others include: any time an inmate leaves the institution for any reason, for example for a medical appointment; when an external work party is returning to the institution;

and, when an incident in the institution gives rise to the belief an inmate is carrying an illegal item. If having accepted that being strip-searched is not a pleasurable experience, you are still not persuaded about the potentially bruising nature of life in prison and are thinking that the answer for the inmates is simply to stay out of trouble in order to avoid being searched, there is another piece of prison policy you need to know about.

The policies that are in place within prisons to assist in the maintenance of security require a minimum of two searches be undertaken every day in every prison wing or unit. During my time on the prison floor that meant that even if an inmate was very well-behaved, even if they were committed to just putting their head down and getting on with their sentence, if they happened to stroll past an officer at the same time as he or she was realising the day's strip-searches hadn't been done yet, they were likely to find themselves in line for a strip-search. I am told the practice today involves a computer system randomly identifying the inmates to be searched.

As I think back over my experience as a prison officer, I can recall a number of occasions when an inmate was selected for a strip-search not because the officer believed he was carrying an illegal item or presenting a risk to the security of the institution, but because the officer considered the inmate needed to be put in his place. What better way to do it than to require him to take off his clothes with strangers looking on? In some of the searches done with this motivation, the need to ensure the inmate was never completely naked in front of the searching officers was one aspect of the searching procedures that was often overlooked, something that added to the inmate's humiliation.

While it's true the inmates weren't averse to my seeing them naked in circumstances such as those described in the previous chapter, it is an entirely different situation when there is no choice involved and the need for an inmate to take off his or her clothes is based solely on the need to demonstrate power and control. It didn't happen often, but it did happen. It was for me then, and still is now, a salutary reminder of the absolute powerlessness an inmate experiences while in prison, something those entering Christchurch Women's Prison to view the theatre performance struggled with when required to give up their handbags.

It is true that those choosing to offend are to a significant degree choosing the reality of prison, including strip-searches, and we will come to discuss the degree of choice that is present in due course. What it is important to focus on at this point is the degree to which a prison, any prison, regardless of its outward appearance and the number of bars visible, can seriously be considered a holiday camp when the maintenance of security requires total invasion of an individual's personal space. We also need to focus on what it says about our society, about life in our communities, when a person would deliberately choose to return to prison and suffer the accompanying personal indignities rather than live outside the prison with the rest of us.

In recent years many people have suggested to me that it is a sad commentary on the effectiveness of a term of imprisonment in terms of deterrence from offending that having experienced the reality of prison, so many offenders choose to return, many of them a number of times. On the contrary, I believe it is a comment on us, and our community, that a person would make that choice, seeing prison with all its personal indignities as the preferred option in comparison to the life they can live outside the prison walls. Who would deliberately choose prison and why — these are the questions we need to keep asking.

The call has been made again and again in recent times to make prisons tougher places than they currently are, to feed inmates less, to subject them to hard physical labour and ensure inmates surrender all personal rights. On 12 January 2001, Garth McVicar, Chairman of the Sensible Sentencing Trust, appeared on television to make a response to the revelation that Dartelle Alder, the man convicted of running down and raping jogger Margaret Baxter in January 2000, was being held in a medium-security prison.

On television Mr McVicar made a statement to the effect that he and the other members of the Trust wanted Alder to 'do the sentence in harsh conditions', suggesting that such treatment by the state was merited given the nature of the crime. I don't deny the crime was horrific, it was, and the ongoing pain and grief being experienced by the family and friends of Margaret Baxter in the aftermath of her senseless and violent death cannot be quantified. But what we need to be clear about in debates such as the one about the conditions in which Alder should be held in prison is that offenders are sent to prison *as* punishment, not *for* punishment. The punishment is the removal of the offender's liberty, their personal freedom. When we pursue the idea of harsh treatment of offenders while they are in prison, we are talking about vengeance, not punishment, and if, as a society, we decide we want to move in that direction, we need to be very clear about the likely implications for us all.

To clarify my point about the punishment being the loss of personal freedom, I would like to take you on a short journey.

We are going to one of the top hotels in Auckland and you will check into the penthouse suite. You will be living, free of charge, in very luxurious surroundings. Once you have checked in, you will be told you are to remain in the hotel until further notice. You have access to room service and can order anything you wish with no limit in terms of cost. As a general rule, once a day someone will unlock the door of your suite and you will be given some time to mix with the residents of the adjoining suite. The time of day you are unlocked and the amount of time you have to mix with others will depend on hotel routines; you will have no control over this. Some days will pass without the door being unlocked and if you ask about that and your entitlement to have some time out of your suite, you will be told that hotel routines didn't permit it that day. You have no redress against the decision. Apart from the restriction in terms of the amount of time you can spend out of your suite, you are completely free and you can do whatever you want in your room. The main restriction is you cannot go home — you *cannot* leave.

For some who are reading this, I will have just provided a description of heaven. To no longer have to be anywhere by a certain time, to have the freedom to do anything you want, to lie in bed all day watching videos, reading books and ordering in delicious meals and nice wine — heaven indeed given the frenetic lives most of us lead. But regardless of how good it feels at the beginning, I think I can guarantee that even for the more severely stressed among you, it wouldn't be long before the appeal of the situation began to pall and you would want to go home.

Within a reasonably short period of time, you would begin to lose interest in being able to sleep, watch videos, read and order in great food. You would begin to resent the degree to which your life was being controlled by someone else and would become angry about your inability to control, or even know in advance, how long you were going to be allowed out of your room in the days ahead. You would begin to long for the simple pleasures of life, such as choosing to go for a walk or to a movie, and you would yearn for the return of your personal freedom.

That is prison.

It doesn't matter how well you are fed, how soft the bed is or whether you get the chance to watch television — the reality is that your life is completely controlled by someone else. They tell you when to get up, when to go to bed, when to eat, when to work and when to stand in front of them and take off your clothes. They decide for security reasons that the day's work out in the prison garden you thought you had in front of you isn't going to happen. Instead you spend the day locked in your cell or sitting in a concrete yard with a number other inmates, some of whom seem quite keen on making your life a misery for no other reason than that they are bored or they don't like the shape of your face. You have no recourse and demanding your rights isn't going to improve your situation; instead, it's far more likely to annoy both the other inmates and the staff. And if you continue to demand your rights and argue the toss with prison staff, you may well find your freedom within the prison curtailed even more.

In the worst-case scenario, arguing with an officer can lead to you facing an internal disciplinary charge for offending against good order and discipline and your release date from prison may be affected. You are quite literally on a hiding to nothing and inmates survive best in prison once they have accepted that reality and resolved to simply get on with their sentence. We don't need to humiliate them any further. There is adequate humiliation involved in the daily routines of the institution. In the blunt words of one male inmate: 'You can't even have a shit without having to ask for toilet paper.'

While acknowledging the professionalism of the majority of the custodial staff who work in our prisons, the reality is that they tell an inmate to jump and the only appropriate response from the inmate is to ask how high. In effect an inmate becomes the property of the justice system.

It doesn't matter that the inmate can look out the window of their cell and see green grass and blue sky or that they get to walk outside in the fresh air regularly. It doesn't matter that they are fed reasonably good quality food three times a day or that they can have a television set in their cell if their family is able to provide one. They wake up in their cell at 4 a.m. and know they cannot leave the space in which they are confined until some-one decides to unlock the door. They know in those lonely early morning hours that every aspect of the life they will lead until the end of their sentence arrives will be controlled by someone else. And they know that the fact they are in prison means they are considered worthless by those who sit on the other side of the fence.

That is prison.

When I entered the world of women offenders at Christchurch Women's Prison, I gained another perspective on the question of why a person would consider prison, with all its personal indignities and complete lack of personal autonomy, a preferable option to life outside the prison gates.

I learned through my contact with many of the women in Christchurch Women's that the sad reality for many women, and no doubt also for a number of men, is that prison is the only place they can feel truly safe. When the door of the cell is finally locked behind them and the area in which they are living shrinks to a concrete space the sides of which they can touch if they stretch out their arms, for the first time in their lives, they experience a feeling of safety and sense of control over their own destiny. In the words of one female inmate: 'When you hear the key turn at night, you know it's night-time and you've got 10 hours to yourself.'

These are people who have never known what it is to have a sense of personal space; people whose bodies were not their own from as young as two or three years of age, with those around them using their bodies for gratification without hesitation. These are people who have their personal radar running permanently in an attempt to avoid further abuse, to avoid getting into trouble and getting the inevitable hiding.

When the cell door closes behind her or him and they know no one is coming in again until the general unlock in 10 hours time, for possibly the first time in their life they can turn the radar off and relax. Little wonder they choose prison.

For the average female inmate, the world is a dangerous place, a place that continually assaults her in every way imaginable — physically, psychologically and sexually. She comes to prison and for a time there is a sense of peace, a peace not even the indignities of prison life can penetrate. Life has never been good to her; the level of abuse having to be endured the only thing that has varied as she has grown up. The personal humiliation she suffers in prison is preferable to what awaits her in the outside world. The question for those who seek to make prisons tougher places, places where inmates are reminded with even greater force than they are now of their worthlessness, is whether we are willing to allow the state to take up the role of abuser where the abusers in many of the inmates' lives have left off.

To advocate that prisons as they exist now are harsh enough places regardless of their outward appearance is not to undermine the pain and grief of the victims of crime. The ways in which Margaret Baxter, Kylie Jones, James Whakaruru and Tangaroa Matui, among others, died were horrific and no excuses can be made for the perpetrators of the violent acts that led to their deaths. They did the crime and they certainly need to do the time.

I freely acknowledge that were one of my children to be harmed or killed in a similar fashion, I am sure I wouldn't be entirely rational in determining the punishment I would like to see meted out to the offender. I also know that whatever punishment was imposed, it would be unlikely to satisfy my need for revenge or ease my pain. While I can acknowledge my humanity in this respect, however, my time working with offenders has left me with more questions than answers with regard to how best to impact societal change in terms of the increasing level of violent crime in our communities. I remain unconvinced that vengeance or state-sanctioned brutality within prisons, such as that seeming to be advocated by many of those who support tougher sentences, is the answer.

When I entered the probation service a lifetime ago, I saw the world as a reasonably black and white place — good and bad, right and wrong, crime and punishment. The fact I held such views was no doubt due in part to my age and in part to my white middle-class Catholic upbringing. Some of my life experience had left me with the sense there was some grey between the large chunks of black and white, but only a little. And then life caught up with me. The more I interacted with offenders, the more insight I gained into the tangled web that was life for most of them.

The more I looked into their offending and the reasons that lay behind it, the more I was unable to self-righteously condemn them. I found that while I wasn't prepared, nor was I required, to excuse their offending, I was beginning to understand how and why life had gone so horribly wrong for them. As one inmate said when talking about his journey to prison: 'Something happened to me when I was young and my wairua went away and stayed away for a long time.'

Another piece of learning in this regard occurred when I became the mother of teenagers. I can still recall the vulnerability that stage of parenting involved, the sense that it didn't matter how well I thought I had done 'the parenting thing' until that point, it was now a case of crossing my fingers and hoping they would make it through. As I patrolled the prison wings as my son approached adolescence and noted the number of young men who had come to prison in the course of attempting to prove to the world that they were adults totally in control of their own destiny, I began to more fully understand the phrase 'there but for the grace of God'. Sixteen years after my entry into the world of criminal offending, I am now of the view that the world is made up of very small chunks of black and white in the middle of an enormous area of grey.

While the violent death of a defenceless child at the hands of someone who is supposed to love and protect them can never be excused, I am no longer sure where to direct the anger I inevitably feel when I discover that the perpetrator was himself a badly abused child, one who in some ways had the misfortune to survive a childhood of neglect, deprivation and abuse and live long enough to become an abuser.

If the issue is the need for offenders sentenced to a term of imprisonment to own their crime and acknowledge its effect on the lives of their victims, it is my belief that there is a far more effective option open to us than that of seeking to make prisons more barbaric places than they already are. My experience with the theatre productions at Christchurch Women's Prison showed me the answer doesn't lie in brutality and vengeance, but rather in the creation of a vacuum within which the inmate comes face

73

to face with themselves, the crime they have committed and the victims they have created. Again and again, as the inmates taking part in the productions wrestled with the pain involved in taking off the many-layered masks they had habitually worn to keep themselves safe and stop themselves feeling in the world, they spoke of how much easier it would be to simply resume the wearing of the masks and return to the mainstream prison routines rather than continuing with the journey into their past.

The majority of offenders come to prison with their lives in chaos. A significant number will have been in institutions of one sort or another for a substantial period of their lives. Many are abuse victims who have suffered a level of abuse from when they were small children, the scale of which we cannot even begin to imagine, and some of the younger inmates now arriving at the prison gates have been living on the streets and engaging in prostitution since they were 12 or 13 years of age.

The reality we have to come to grips with is that the idea the system might be able to subdue these people and persuade them through tougher sentences that they should cease offending is a nonsense. Put simply, there is nothing the system can do to them that hasn't already been done. Treating them badly doesn't lead them to make a decision to cease re-offending and turn their life around; it just hardens their heart against the world a little more each time it happens, reminding them that those who have the power win, and so the possibility of yet another victim is created. In the words of one young inmate: 'Making inmates do a harder time, all you are going to get is a harder inmate released on the street as your neighbour. What's the point in making young people madder and madder?'

In the lead-up to each of the two Arts Festival productions, the Te Rakau Hua drama troupe worked with the inmates taking part for a total of three months before the performance was considered ready for a public audience. During that time, there were many occasions when it was possible to see inmates struggling with the honesty that was required of them as they travelled back through their lives to the point where, as Jim Moriarty put it, 'their spirit was first hurt'. For some it was almost too difficult and at times when the pain threatened to overwhelm them, they would stand on the brink of disobeying one of the institution rules and pause, almost as if they wanted to be charged with an breach of the rules which would mean being withdrawn from the performance.

I have seen a number of inmates work well in prison programmes and make significant progress in coming to terms with the impact of their offending on themselves, their family and their victims, only to deliberately assault another inmate or an officer and be punished accordingly. Rather than being upset at the imposition of a sentence of solitary confinement, they have appeared relaxed and have readily accepted the consequences of their actions. When asked why they committed the offence that saw them backtrack in their sentence, some have been able to articulate that they prefer the environment of the separates, where the rules are overt and no one hassles them about their life or the reason they are in prison, to a situation where they have to unravel the tangled web of their past.

They know brutality, they know deprivation and they sit comfortably with them. If we really want to shift them outside their comfort zone and make them face the consequences of their actions, we need to be creating a space around them that allows them to come face to face with themselves, own their crime, grieve about the life into which they were born and move on.

A number of young children have died violent deaths at the hands of a parent in recent years in New Zealand. One inmate I have worked with was responsible for one of these deaths. In discussions I have had with members of the public about the conditions in which prison inmates are held, it hasn't been uncommon for people to suggest ways in which I might make the life of this inmate more difficult and so exact greater retribution for the death of the child. My view is quite different.

If the prison system does what it needs to with this inmate in the course of the sentence of imprisonment, the inmate will grow ever closer to a full realisation of the part she played in the death of her child. The creation of this awareness is not something that can happen overnight, but it is something that can and will happen if the right steps are taken. Nothing you or I might do to her, nothing the system might do in terms of trying to increase the punishment to a level where it is felt the child's death will be avenged can compare to the pain this inmate will feel at the moment she comes to the full realisation of the part she played in the death of her child. And once she has reached that level of awareness, she will live with it forever.

In my mind, that is the real punishment — full ownership of the crime and the consequences of that crime. That is what will allow us to begin to make real progress in addressing the increasing levels of violence in our communities. That is what will allow us to begin to feel hopeful again about the world that awaits our children and grandchildren.

5: So what about cannabis?

Alcohol and drugs are significant factors in the journey taken to prison by the majority of prison inmates. In my view, a conservative estimate would be that approximately 80–85 per cent of the inmates resident in New Zealand prisons have a history of addiction to alcohol and/or drugs. Prison happens for a great many inmates either when they have committed a crime while totally 'off their face', when they are under the influence of alcohol or drugs to the extent that they have no idea where they are or what they are doing, or when their need for alcohol or drugs is such that they will do anything to get the money they need to satisfy their craving.

While I do not intend to discuss in any real depth the issue of drugs in prison, I will say at the outset that at various times over the years, I have found the community's outrage at the idea inmates are able to gain access to illicit drugs in prison intriguing. At certain points when this has been a topical issue, for example when there has been discussion about new measures being taken to control the flow of drugs into prison, the discussion in the media has almost gone as far as to suggest prison authorities were at worst complicit in the acceptance of drug use in the institutions in the country, or at best ineffective in their attempts to control it. Nothing could be further from the truth. A great deal of energy is spent trying to ensure illicit drugs are not readily available to inmates in prison and significant success is achieved in this regard due to the efforts of very dedicated and diligent prison staff. The vital piece of the puzzle that seems to be missing in terms of the community's understanding of the issue is just how easy it is to get drugs into prison, especially given the extremely high motivation of the inmates to do so.

Staying with the statistic of 80–85 per cent of prison inmates having a drug and/or alcohol addiction, that means there are a great many inmates who, when they arrive in prison, are going to go through a very abrupt detoxification process. A major component of the reception of an inmate into prison can be management of his or her withdrawal from the wide range of substances they were regularly using in the days, weeks and months prior to being sentenced. Another component of their reception can be determining what they might have hidden in various crevices in their body in anticipation of the fact they were likely to receive a term of imprisonment when they appeared in court. Once the initial withdrawal process has been survived and the prison sentence kicks in, the inmate is faced with the reality that they are going to have to get through each day without chemical support. In that moment life can become a terrifying thing.

In my experience, nine times out of ten the fundamental issue behind an inmate's use of alcohol or drugs will be their desperate need to forget the reality of their lives. The use of various substances allows them to submerge the memories of the abuse they have suffered most of their lives and lose, for a brief moment, their ever-present sense of being unloved and unwanted. When 'she' sticks the needle in her arm, she can forget for the next little while what it felt like as the sweat from his chin dripped onto her face as he raped her, he being a 30-year-old man, she being an 8-year-old child. They also use the substances to alleviate their ever-present sense that they are failing at life. In that, they aren't too different to the rest of us really, only somehow the drugs we use to combat our fear and vulnerability in life are rationalised as being more acceptable, as are our reasons for using them.

Given the desperation involved and the scale of their need to forget, it isn't surprising that inmates who have to come clean not out of choice, but because they have been sentenced to a term of imprisonment, will go to almost any lengths to obtain illicit drugs while in prison including, as recent media reports suggest, using children as smuggling agents. When you also realise that enough tablets to keep the inmate 'happy' for quite some time (tablets that will be melted down and injected to achieve maximum impact) can be wrapped in a piece of clingfilm and comprise a parcel no bigger than a third of the fingernail on your little finger, the difficulty involved in keeping drugs out of prison begins to take on realistic proportions.

During my term as manager of Christchurch Women's Prison, I entered a debate with members of the Christchurch community about the idea of putting women convicted of illicit drug use within the prison into overalls for visits. The idea was that overalls zipped up the back and securely fastened at the neck, wrists and ankles would limit the opportunities for the inmates to internally secrete drugs brought in by their visitors before being searched at the conclusion of the visit. In the initial stages of the debate, I took quite a bit of heat for what was seen as a barbaric idea. The reality for me as the manager of the prison was that although I would have preferred not to have had to treat women obviously severely addicted to drugs in that way, on the very morning the public meeting I had called to discuss the issue was held, I received the results of a urine test undertaken by an inmate who had been suspected of using drugs in the institution. The test had revealed traces of three illicit drugs in her system; cannabis, benzodiazepine and heroin.

In my view, we were lucky she was still alive and I believed I had an obligation to try to manage her access to illicit drugs better if she was ever going to come to grips with her addiction, and not die from a drug overdose in a backstreet alley.

An interesting challenge was issued at the public meeting by one of the two local kuia who worked to support Maori women in the prison, a wonderful woman with incredible wisdom who added much value in her work within the prison. After listening to the criticism being offered about how the prison was managing the issue of illicit drug use among inmates, she stood and made the point that it wasn't prison management those at the meeting concerned about the treatment of inmates should be focusing on. She noted that the inmates required the cooperation of members of the community outside the prison walls to access a supply of illicit drugs and suggested it was the community who should bear primary responsibility for the fact the availability of drugs in prison was an ongoing problem.

She's right. Illicit drugs can only get into prisons with the cooperation of members of the community outside the prison walls, a fact that should give at least a little food for thought. For my part, I would be happy if the community would just add this fact into the debate the next time they have the inclination to criticise prison staff and management for what is seen as their failure to control the flow of drugs into prison.

In thinking about the importation of drugs into prison and the capacity women in particular have to secrete drugs internally, I can recall a delightful conversation I had with one prison manager. As a newly appointed prison inspector, I was trying to come to grips with the differences between male and female inmates in terms of their management within the prison environment. The woman concerned had managed a women's prison for quite some time and was an absolute delight. She was a gentle soul with a length of steel in her spine that only became visible when she was riled about something. She rarely swore, while I had developed the habit of swearing far too often, and she had been working in the system long enough to know running at brick walls was a futile exercise. This meant that in some of the discussions we had as I railed against what I saw as the male system, she just smiled and reflected that there was more than one way to skin a cat.

On this particular day, we were discussing the fact that many of the women in prison seemed to have developed a real skill in internally secreting prohibited items quickly and efficiently.

We chatted for a few moments about the difficulty involved in catching the women out in this regard and I expressed my surprise at the size of a bag of cannabis one inmate had recently been caught with. Given that prison officers are not permitted to do searches of body cavities, her attempts to smuggle the cannabis into the institution would have gone unchecked but for a small piece of plastic showing between her legs. When the inmate finally complied with the request made by the officers undertaking the search to extract the piece of plastic, she removed a large plastic bag containing, as the incident report written subsequently by the officer said, 'a substantial amount of green plant material that appeared to be cannabis'.

When I mentioned my surprise at the size of the plastic bag involved, the prison manager just smiled and made the comment (in exactly the same tone in which the nuns at school used to speak when sharing with us how young ladies were supposed to act): 'Dear, I've known women who could turn an articulated truck around up there.'

While alcohol and a variety of drugs play a significant part in the journey taken to prison by a great number of those who arrive at the prison gates, I have decided to focus the remainder of this discussion about drugs on cannabis. My decision to do so is based on the increasing anger I feel at the manner in which the magic contained inside many of the children born in this country is being bled away by their early and ongoing exposure to cannabis. I am also angered by the degree to which the harm being done to children in this regard is minimised by those who would have us believe the issue underlying the debate about the decriminalisation of cannabis is one of an individual's personal freedom.

I believe I have a good grasp of the concept of personal freedom, and on many occasions in the past have stood to defend an individual's right to choose how they live, what work they undertake and what substances they put into their bodies. However, when it comes to cannabis use within our communities, I don't believe the issue can just be about personal freedom any more. From what I have seen and continue to see, it is now about the destruction of children's lives before they have even really begun.

Early in 2001, I attended a public meeting in Nelson called by Nick Smith, the local Member of Parliament and a member of the National Party, to discuss the possible decriminalisation of cannabis. His fellow guest at the meeting was Nandor Tanczos, also a Member of Parliament and a member of the Green Party.

For quite some time, I sat silently in the meeting (a rare occurrence for me, some would say) and listened as the debate swirled around me. What became clear as the meeting progressed was that a great deal of the debate was focusing on an intellectual analysis of the issue. There was debate about how much harm the drug actually did; about the rights of individuals to decide their own destiny and choose what substances they put in their bodies; about how decriminalising the drug would free up money that could then be spent more effectively in cleaning up the consequences of drug abuse; and, about how much more damaging alcohol abuse is in both health and societal terms. The views expressed at the meeting were similar to those I have often seen expressed in the media and it cannot be denied that they are very convincing arguments when taken at face value.

What also became apparent at the meeting was that those who stood to express their concern at the possible decriminalisation of cannabis were predominantly those who were seeing the consequences of the abuse of the drug firsthand; teachers, health workers, community workers. These people spoke with conviction about the damage they regularly saw being done to young minds and young bodies, damage that was directly attributable to the use of cannabis by the child or young person or to the use of the drug by someone significant in their lives.

It is a great topic for a debate — the degree to which the state has the right to dictate how we live, what we eat, what we inject, what we smoke. But that isn't the debate we need to be having as the crime rate grows and as the age at which young girls and boys are becoming prostitutes on the streets of our major cities drops to single figures. The debate we need to be having now concerns the degree to which the use of cannabis is impacting negatively on the future of our children and contributing to the ever growing number of young people being admitted to our prisons.

I quite frankly don't give a damn if an adult somewhere in New Zealand wants to enjoy the personal freedom of being able to light up a joint at the end of the day and in certain circumstances, I would probably defend that person's right to do so. What I do give a damn about is the child who from three months of age regularly has cannabis smoke blown up his nose because his young and woefully ill-equipped mother has no idea how else to stop his incessant crying and has no one in her life willing and able to suggest other options in the moments of stress she regularly experiences. What I do give a damn about are the number of young children who live lives of transience and disconnection from mainstream society because their parents are focused not on the wellbeing of their children, but on their need to live in an area where cannabis is readily available and a certain degree of distance can be maintained from the authorities.

There are children in this country who have been enrolled in excess of 15 primary schools before their tenth birthday because their parents need to keep on the move, keep away from official attention and go where cannabis is easy to access. There are children who come to primary school on a Monday morning stoned and unable to take in any of the information being presented by the teacher because they have spent the weekend inhaling cannabis smoke in the family home as an all-weekend party went on around them.

A number of teachers have spoken to me about how they have had to accept that some students won't take anything in until the Wednesday of each school week, because it takes that long for them to come out of the drug stupor either passive or active smoking of cannabis over the weekend in the family home has induced. They are having to alter their teaching methods to accommodate this reality. And they're not talking about secondary school students.

I don't claim to know the answer to the drug problem that currently exists in our communities. It is possible the decriminalisation of cannabis could be part of the solution, but only if we could be sure the resources that would be freed up if the police and the court system didn't have to deal with cannabis offences were able to be directed towards making a difference in the lives of those who suffer the consequences of drug abuse. I remain sceptical of that happening, as I don't believe enough people have a sense of how pervasive the destruction being wreaked in the communities around New Zealand is, but it is one possible option that remains available to us.

I might not know the answer to the drug problem, but there are some things I do know. I know the debate I have seen and heard to date on the issue of the decriminalisation of cannabis is heavily impacted by middle-class values and attitudes and by concerns for the maintenance of individual personal freedom. It has little to do with the reality being lived by many of the children in our society. And I do know that if the use of drugs like cannabis leads to a person committing an offence and being sentenced to a term of imprisonment, the majority of people in the community seem comfortable with the idea that the person's addiction is of their own making and they should suffer the consequences of their actions, regardless of how their addiction came about.

At the meeting in Nelson I have spoken of, I was concerned to note the hero-like status with which Nandor Tanczos was received at the meeting by a large group of young people, who had obviously come to see him champion the cause of the decriminalisation of cannabis.

Let me be clear. I have no interest in whether Nandor does or does not smoke cannabis; he is an adult, he knows the effects of the drug, both long-term and short-term, and he is well able to accept the consequences of any choice he makes. Having watched the reception he received at the meeting, however, I was left with some concerns about the flow-on effect of having a Member of Parliament openly champion the cause of a substance known to do substantial damage to the brains of young children.

The young people who had come to see Nandor were like all young people throughout the generations. They were keen to pin their hopes and aspirations on someone who has demonstrated their ability to thumb their nose at the system, stand up for what they believe in and show a little civil disobedience along the way. In Nandor they had found the perfect hero. He was a member of the establishment, had found his way into Parliament, the perceived seat of power in the country, and yet he wears his hair in dreadlocks and openly admits to regularly smoking cannabis, a drug deemed by the system to be illegal.

A number of the young people in the group appeared to be in their late teens or early twenties and I was comfortable that they should be free to make their choices about the use of cannabis. But others appeared significantly younger, and were obviously being swept along by their older associates. As I watched the fervour Nandor stirred among the group whenever he spoke of the decriminalisation of cannabis and noted the mocking tone that same group adopted towards anyone at the meeting who spoke of the negative effects of cannabis, I couldn't help but think about the children whose lives have been blighted by the drug from a very early age, before they could exercise their right to choose. And I couldn't help but think about some of the discussions I had engaged in with secondary school students about the effect of cannabis on their lives.

Young people today are faced with major life decisions at an increasingly early age. There may be increased freedom for us all, children included, but it comes with a cost. The world is potentially a more harmful place and the stakes are higher than they were when I, and many of you reading this book, were children. There is a wider range of illicit drugs available and they are more lethal. There are sexually transmitted diseases that can kill you rather than just require a dose of penicillin. Children growing up in today's world need robust decision-making ability if they are going to be able to keep themselves safe as they find their way into adulthood. They are dependent on the adults in their lives and the adults they aspire to be like to help them to develop that decision-making ability.

In terms of cannabis use, many young people with whom I have interacted in recent times have articulately described the difficulties they have encountered in trying to evaluate the evidence and make the right decision in terms of whether they should or shouldn't use the drug. It was interesting to note in the discussions that the average age at which the majority of children today seem to be faced with making this decision is 13 or 14 years of age. I'm not sure many parents realise their children are faced with making this particular decision quite so young. (For some children the moment of decision-making comes even earlier.) I have had it suggested to me many times by adults that only children in lower socioeconomic areas have access to drugs in their early teens. But the young people who spoke to me, many of whom claimed to be regular cannabis users who first smoked in their initial year at secondary school, were predominantly middle-class youngsters whose discussion about their lives suggested they came from stable family homes.

When their cannabis use was discussed with these young people, they often spoke of their decision to use the drug being influenced by the hypocrisy of many of the potential role models in their world, teachers, police and the like. These people regularly stated both to the young people themselves, and in public forums, that young people should avoid using cannabis because of its potential harm, while they themselves were long-time and often blatant users of the drug. It seemed to me, as I spoke with these young people, that the 'do as we say, not as we do' adage applied by adults to children of my generation was still out there. However, the old adage took no account of the way in which the world has changed in recent times, or of the dangers children today face from an early age.

I am neither a scientist nor a doctor and I don't believe I would acquit myself particularly well in a debate about cannabis that focused only on whether it can be proven in scientific terms to damage the bodies and minds of those who use it. Scientific proof aside, however, over the past 16 years I have watched the dreams, hopes and aspirations of countless young men and women with enormous potential literally go up in smoke as they have succumbed to the inertia that appears to come with addiction to regular cannabis use. I cannot be dispassionate about it and wait for the irrefutable scientific proof. I know children's lives are being ruined. I know those damaged children don't go away; they eventually appear in our prisons and our psychiatric institutions, having done harm to themselves or another human being. And I know that it's not enough for the rest of us to simply consider drug addiction to be the problem of those who are addicted.

On 8 March 2002 the *Dominion* newspaper ran a front-page story under the headline 'Cannabis poisons toddlers'. According to the story, 33 children under the age of two and a half have been admitted to North Island hospitals with cannabis poisoning in the past six years. Given the degree to which the symptoms can go unrecognised, the paediatrician stated that it was possible up to 100 children each year were admitted to hospital with cannabis poisoning. These are children whose lives have not even really begun, children who, as a result of having been exposed to cannabis, suffer muscles spasms or go into a coma, some requiring admission into intensive care. They will probably be lucky enough to recover physically, but there has to be a strong chance they will be damaged psychologically in ways we can only guess.

For those of us concerned at the idea that children so young are being affected by cannabis, it isn't enough to simply condemn their parents and return to our coffee and newspaper. Nor is it enough to say in response to the revelation that adult prison visitors are reportedly using children to smuggle drugs into prisons that prison authorities need to clamp down further on drug use in prisons. The harsh reality is that it isn't 'their' problem any more; whether we like it or not, it has become 'our' problem. If we have any hope for the future of this country, uncomfortable as it may be, we have to begin to make the connections, to be willing to understand what is now a very complex issue in terms of its potential societal impact.

In the aftermath of the Knowledge Wave conference held in Auckland in 2001, Ian Taylor, Managing Director of Animation Research Ltd, wrote an article for the *Dominion* newspaper that appeared in print on 10 September 2001. In the article Ian suggests that getting ahead is all about attitude and asks the question that if we are serious about becoming a knowledge economy, 'how is it that we could even begin to contemplate decriminalising a drug (cannabis) that has so much potential to damage young brains?' I'm with Ian, although from my perspective it isn't totally about whether to decriminalise or not to decriminalise. It is about making the connections. What good does it do to hold talk fests about how to make this country great again and encourage the return of the pioneer spirit we were once so famous for, when we fail to recognise the degree to which the future potential of the country is being limited by cannabis use among our young people, all of our young people, not just those we are willing to lose?

We tell ourselves the drug problem belongs with those who use the drugs and when drug use leads to the imposition of a term of imprisonment, we shake our heads and agree it is terrible someone was hurt or killed, but continue to refuse to accept that some of those who are in prison took their first steps on the path to addiction and prison when their father blew cannabis smoke up their nose when they were three, as a party trick.

Offenders commit offences and they need to accept responsibility for their actions, but we have a responsibility too.

'He' may have chosen to do the burglary, but he did so while under the influence of a mind-altering substance he became addicted to after being encouraged to share a joint with his father when he was six. 'She' may have chosen to do the home invasion that led to an old man being stabbed, but she did so in a desperate attempt to find some money for the drugs she had become addicted to while working on the streets of Auckland as a child prostitute, regularly sought out by men eager to have sex with a child.

Decriminalisation may be one part of the answer, but a bigger part must be education of those who are raising children considered at risk about the dangers of cannabis use. It isn't an easy problem, but it is our problem and belongs to us all regardless of the strata of society from which we come. It may be about a need to ensure some people have the opportunity to learn better parenting skills, but it is also about each of us knowing our children and grandchildren are not immune to the dangers of drug use. It isn't just about an individual's right to choose; it is also about children not being given a chance in life. It isn't just about people coming to terms with their addiction and working to change their lives in order to be considered valid members of our society; it is also about our children, grandchildren and great grandchildren and the future we want for them here in New Zealand.

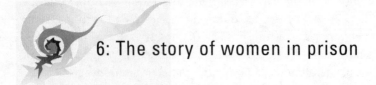

6: The story of women in prison

Early in March 2002, there were approximately 5200 offenders in prison in New Zealand and of that number, approximately 225 were women. Traditionally in all western countries women comprise approximately 5 per cent of the general prison population. The obvious question that poses itself in the face of these statistics is what such a substantial difference in numbers indicates in terms of women's offending. The initial answer I like to give to that question, particularly in a room full of men, is that women are obviously smarter than men, planning their offences better and not getting caught as often. While such an answer always gets a great response from women (and a slightly less positive reaction from men), the truth behind the variance in the figures is a little more complex. I do not intend to provide a complete list of possible reasons for the variance, but some discussion might help set the scene as we enter the world of women in prison.

One of the reasons for the lower number of women in prison is that women commit less crime than men. There are several possible explanations for this; less opportunity to do so, given the fact adolescent girls have traditionally had less social freedom than their male counterparts (although this appears to have changed a great deal in recent years); less likelihood of becoming involved in crime as part of the passage into adulthood due to an absence, or at least a limited amount, of peer pressure in that regard; and, a greater ability to determine the link between action and consequence. I am aware there will be people who will consider the latter a sexist remark that denigrates men, but I am commenting solely on the basis of what I observed during the time I spent in prisons. It seemed to me that many of the men I met in prison were more than a little bemused about how they had ended up there. They had 'just been having a bit of fun' and somehow it had all gone horribly wrong and before they knew it, they were in a police cell and on their way to prison. Getting them to see where and how the journey to prison had begun in order that they might begin to consider other paths in life was often quite a difficult task.

The majority of the women I met in prison, on the other hand, appeared either to have taken a calculated risk in doing what they had done, knowing that one of the possible consequences was a term of imprisonment, or to have committed the offence knowing a term of imprisonment was inevitable, but choosing to go ahead and do it anyway.

While the entry to prison of many men appeared almost accidental, the majority of women appeared to have arrived in prison as the result of a conscious choice to act in a certain way.

Another reason for the lower number of women in prison has been linked to societal attitudes about the appropriateness of sending women to prison. Historically, the attitudes of some of those who have been involved in the oversight of women within the criminal justice system have incorporated the view that women are the weaker sex and thus less responsible for their deviant behaviour. This stance has meant that a woman often had to commit a greater number of offences than a man or commit a particularly serious first offence before a term of imprisonment was considered as an option. In the past, community sanctions were considered a more preferable option for women in terms of punishment and as a result women had longer journeys to prison. Things are changing in this regard, however; women are increasingly being held accountable as adults for the crimes they commit rather than being seen simply as 'naughty girls'. The arrival of female and younger male judges on the bench appears to have had an impact in this regard.

In an extension of the difference in sentencing practice described above, it has seemed at times in the past as if the different treatment has been not only about a failure to see women as adults responsible for their behaviour, but also about a reluctance to send women to prison because doing so allowed the women to evade their responsibilities as a mother. The crime was categorised as an aberration in behaviour by a woman whose primary role in life was childcare, rather than being recognised as a deliberate course of action chosen by the woman. Having been suitably chastised, she was then sent back to the family home where she belonged, with appropriate boundaries in place. Things have changed a great deal in recent times, however, and for the better in my view, and it is in part as a result of this change in attitude that the female prison population is growing at a significant rate in New Zealand, as it is around the world.

I see it as one of the positive spin-offs of the feminist movement, that women are being held accountable as fully functioning adults for their actions rather than simply seen as transgressing children who need to learn the correct way to behave. It can only be a good thing that women's criminal behaviour is now being judged on the basis of more objective and less patriarchal criteria. The view of women as transgressing children was still detectable in the women's prisons in New Zealand when I first entered them as a prison inspector in 1994.

In many ways, in comparison to the manner in which male prisons were run, at that time women's prisons were still being run as institutions whose primary function was to teach the occupants how women should behave in society, rather than as prisons. If men's prisons were overgrown boarding schools, women's prisons were finishing schools for those 'girls' who had failed to comply with society's expectations regarding their future. I can still recall how surprised I was when I first had contact with women's prisons to find that women in prison were often referred to and addressed as 'girls' by those involved in their management. As I began to wade into the issue of women in prison and attempt to advocate for them in a system that almost completely ignored their existence, I can remember often challenging that in fact they were not girls, but fully menstruating adult women, and deserved to be recognised as such.

While there have been some positive spin-offs to the change in societal attitudes about women, there has also been at least one negative spin-off. Young women raised in the time of the 'Girls can do anything' bumper sticker, as my daughter was, really do believe that to be the case — they can do anything. And they are. Unfortunately for many young women, that doesn't mean challenging traditionally male work environments such as the police and the fire service or seeking to break the glass ceiling and gain entry to male-dominated management structures within public organisations. Instead it means doing the burglary or home invasion themselves rather than simply going along for the ride when the young men they are mixing with decide to commit the offence.

I have been asked a number of times recently whether I am surprised by statistics that show a marked increase in the amount of crime being committed by women, young women in particular, and my answer has always been and will continue to be no. Why would I, or anyone for that matter, be surprised by this statistic when everywhere we look, we see evidence of the significant changes that have occurred for women in New Zealand in the last two decades? We have a woman as prime minister and a woman in the position of attorney general. Until recently we had a woman leading the opposition and the governor general is a woman, as is the chief justice and the CEO of Telecom.

In the face of this evidence of changing times, we cannot legitimately claim to be surprised by the increase in the amount and seriousness of crime being committed by women. Women are recognised within our society to a significantly greater degree than ever before as autonomous individuals, rather than being held captive by societal expectations that deemed their place to be in the kitchen and the bedroom.

It is this change that has assisted the entry of women into traditionally male environments and if the change in attitude is visible at one end of the spectrum in such glaring terms as those outlined above, why would we not expect to see equally glaring changes at the other end — women becoming freer to commit crime, and more serious crime? Given that the option of becoming the prime minister or the CEO of Telecom is not a viable one for the many women in New Zealand who have had the misfortune to be born into the wrong family, the commission of an offence is often the only way in which they feel they can take some control over their lives and give themselves a sense of identity and purpose.

In terms of the idea that it's a good thing that women be seen as adults fully accountable for their actions, I have no doubt there are some who would argue that a system that seeks to make women fully accountable runs the risk of not recognising the degree to which many women continue to be victimised in our society, despite the progress obviously being made in some areas.

I am not suggesting that victimisation of women no longer occurs or that we shouldn't take account of the very real fact that many women have a limited range of choices available to them as they make their way through life. I am very conscious that it is often the fact that their choices are so limited that influences their decision to commit a crime and risk prison. But at the same time, seeking to excuse women's criminal behaviour on the basis that they are naughty girls and not responsible for what they have done does them no favours. I prefer to work with the idea that these women have deliberately chosen to behave in a certain way, albeit for a reason they feel strongly about, and within a very limited range of choices, and that the next step lies in increasing their awareness of ways in which their range of choices can be increased.

I am passionate about women's prisons and about the women

who reside in them. I am passionate about them because I have been lucky enough to experience firsthand the magic that can happen within women's prisons. Another reason is because I believe women's prisons to be one of the major focal points at which we can and should begin the process of impacting real societal change; change that will lead to a decrease in the number of children whose lives are filled with violence and abuse; a decrease in the number of children who die before their time at the hands of someone who is supposed to love and protect them; and a decrease in the number of families who have to live with the relentless pain of having a family member die in violent and senseless circumstances.

During the three and a half years I worked at Christchurch Women's Prison, and the following year as I wrote a document on the management of women in prison for the Department of Corrections, I was constantly involved in a comparison between the world of men's prisons and that of women's prisons. The need for this comparison had arisen out of the fact that women's prisons in New Zealand were very much the poor relations; they were significantly under-resourced in comparison to their male counterparts and rather than there being any real recognition of the inherent differences between men and women in general and between men and women in the custodial setting, there was a constant frustration detectable among management at various levels that women's prisons wouldn't run like men's prisons. The fact that women's prisons wouldn't run like men's prisons because they were full of women didn't seem to have occurred to those overseeing their management.

The women themselves experienced enormous frustration as they continued to be subject to rules and regulations emanating from decisions made about how best to manage male inmates. It was common practice that when an escape or a major security breach occurred in a men's prison, in the aftermath of the investigation of the incident new policies would be introduced, policies that inevitably involved increased restrictions being placed on all inmates, including the women. The women saw this as blatantly unfair, given that they generally had no interest in escaping or committing security breaches and had done nothing to merit the increased restrictions on their behaviour. The imposition of a blanket restriction on all men in prison as the result of the behaviour of one or a few men was bad enough, but they saw it as particularly unfair that they were drawn into the net as well. I agreed with the women in this regard and felt their frustration, particularly when the consequence of the blanket restriction was inevitably the loss of yet another opportunity to increase the women's chances of successful reintegration back into their families and the community.

I don't intend to repeat what I did while working within the Department of Corrections and describe the world of women's prisons from the perspective of a comparison with the world of men's prisons. I don't intend to do so because I consider women's prisons to be an entity in their own right and believe decisions about how they are run should be based on the reality that is women's prisons, rather than from the perspective of determining what differences to men's prisons are considered valid and acceptable.

However, before I begin my description of the world of women's prisons, it may be useful to describe a few of the ways in which the differences between men and women can manifest in a custodial environment.

The world that opened in front of me as I entered Christchurch Women's Prison was completely different to the world I had left behind at Wi Tako and Ohura Prisons. As I have already described, my time in the male prisons left me with the sense that the majority of male inmates appeared to be boys occupying men's bodies, men whose emotional development had been impaired by the circumstances of their upbringing. In saying that, it is not my intention to suggest all men in prison are emotionally immature. Nor do I wish to downplay the effect of prison on the men or the potential danger of the male prison environment, or to suggest that all men who reside in male prisons are harmless individuals who are just misunderstood. I have looked into the face of evil on more than one occasion during the time I have spent in prisons and more than once I have felt the hairs go up on the back of my neck as I have tuned into the true nature of the person with whom I was interacting.

By and large, however, male prisons impressed me as places where life is simple — the inmates were seeking to do their time and to stay out of trouble to the greatest degree possible. If trouble reached out for them, if their mana was threatened by another inmate or by an officer, they would respond, but very rarely did they seek out trouble or become involved in the affairs of another inmate. A day in which they were not charged with an offence against the prison rules, were fed and had the opportunity to watch a game of rugby or rugby league on television was a good day. This is not how it was in a women's prison.

The things I learned in my first few months at Christchurch Women's Prison are as follows. Everybody does everybody's sentence. No new rule will be obeyed until the reasons behind the rule have been explained . . . to everyone. If the new rule isn't based on sound reasoning, or even if it is, the muttering about the rule will continue long after the women have been told the rule is here to stay. The women affected by the new rule may return three or four times to challenge the reasoning behind it. The loyalties the women have to their male partners come into the prison with them and if a former partner of the man an inmate is now with is in prison, she will happily resolve any 'unfinished business' her partner has with that woman on his behalf. Unfortunately for those who have to manage them, in the minds of the majority of female inmates, a good day in prison is a day in which a new rule was modified, or perhaps even abandoned, as a result of their challenges.

Let me repeat a story I have often told to illustrate the inherent differences between men and women in a custodial environment.

If I was required to take a work party of eight male inmates out to dig a hole in a paddock, I would tell them that's what we were doing and they would dutifully follow me out to the paddock, shovels in hand, and begin digging. They wouldn't need to know what the hole was for nor would they care about the location that had been chosen for the hole. As long as they were allowed to stop every hour for a smoke, they got a cup of tea at smoko time and lunch appeared about the time they started to feel hungry, they would be fine and happily keep digging. Eventually someone might ask: 'What are we doing this for, Boss?' and as long as the answer was not too far-fetched, the digging would continue until they were told the hole was deep enough or the end of the work day arrived. Now let's try that same exercise with a work party of eight female inmates.

Before the women even picked up the shovels, they would want to know where the hole was being dug; what the hole was for; how deep it was to be; who was bringing morning tea; what time they would be stopping for lunch; had anyone thought that the hole would be better in a different place (they have just the place in mind)? Bearing in mind that there hasn't yet been any movement towards the prison gates by the work party, there would then be a discussion about the fact that the shovels were not sharp enough to do the job and that the handles on the shovels were not long enough . . . or were too long.

I can recall telling a group of women at Christchurch Women's Prison this story in an attempt to explain just how much more difficult they were to manage in the prison environment than men. They all had huge grins on their faces as they acknowledged the truth of what I was saying and added that if or when I had answered all the questions they had asked about the digging of the hole, they would then put paid to the idea that they were actually going to do what was being asked of them by telling me that in their view it was men's work!

For all that I found the women in prison more difficult to manage than the men I had previously been involved with, I never lost the sense of pure delight in working in the women's prison environment — a feeling I developed soon after my arrival at the gates of Christchurch Women's Prison. They might have led me to want to tear my hair out at times and I can certainly recall moments when I was very focused on the idea of closing my office door for a moment or two and screaming at the top of my lungs, but the moments of magic far outweighed the moments of frustration.

So what is the reality of women's prisons? Why do I use words like 'delight' and 'magic' in relation to women's prisons and why do I have such a strong belief in women's prisons as one of the major focal points at which we can and should begin to impact real societal change in terms of our high rates of imprisonment, youth suicide and child abuse?

For many of the women who come to prison, the only real alternative to prison is death. Had they not been sentenced to prison, the chances of them dying from a drug overdose, at the hands of their violent partner or at the hands of one of the men willing to pay them for sex, something they tolerate to support their drug habit, are high. They come to prison not as part of the process of growing up, but because their lives have reached a point of total chaos and nothing is working. Their life has finally folded in on itself. They don't come willingly; they come kicking and screaming, convinced that their life is fine and claiming they don't need to be there, they just need the world, the police, whoever, to leave them alone. They tell themselves they have been a good parent to their children, despite what anyone says and they blame the justice system for tearing them away from those children.

Their state of health is appalling. They are addicted to drugs and have a drug of choice, but in an attempt to stave off their ever-present sense of imminent danger and to ensure the memories of their past don't gain a foothold in their conscious mind, they will and do use any mind-altering substance they can get their hands on. They haven't had the time, the energy or the inclination to focus on themselves in the fight for survival that takes place every single day. As a result, they often haven't noticed that they haven't had a period for a few months or they're losing too much weight. They haven't eaten well for some time and are malnourished and run down, their attention having been focused on providing food for their children and acquiring the drugs that will allow them to maintain at least the illusion of control over their increasingly chaotic lives. This isn't every woman who arrives in prison, but it is representative of a great many of them.

As I have said, they haven't come to prison willingly. They have come convinced that the world is against them, they were doing just fine and if the system had just left them alone, all would have been well. They often present as extremely angry women and that anger manifests in aggressive and highly manipulative behaviour within the wings of the prison. I have had the experience of running head-on into that anger in the first few weeks of a number of inmates' sentences.

In some instances when the inmate had been using a needle to inject drugs prior to her entry to prison it was possible, in some of the verbal exchanges that took place between the inmate and I as we settled into each other's space, to quite literally see the serpent sitting behind the inmate's eyes, waiting to strike.

I am aware it isn't a pleasant picture I am constructing and it is often not a pleasant experience for those involved in the first few weeks, or even the first few months, as a woman settles into her sentence. But then you go behind the scenes and begin to build the picture of the life the woman has led prior to her arrival in prison in an attempt to better understand why she presents as she does, and the overwhelming sense you are left with is of one of total surprise — surprise that the woman you are looking at is still alive. Some of the women in prison, many in fact, are miracles simply by virtue of the fact that they are alive, that against all odds they continue to draw air into their lungs. Such has been the range of negative experiences in their lives that it would be totally understandable if they were to choose to lie down and not get up again, or to choose to ensure the drugs they were about to inject had the capacity to make sure they would never wake up. In continuing to choose life, I believe these women are demonstrating a level of courage and resilience that far outweighs anything I have ever been required to face in my life and it is for this reason my primary feeling for them is one of admiration.

When working with Jim Moriarty and his drama troupe, Te Rakau Hua o te Wao Tapu, in preparation for the Christchurch Arts Festival's production of 'Watea — Pathways to Freedom' to be staged at Christchurch Women's Prison in July 1999, the women involved were given the very difficult task of unravelling their personal histories and returning to the moment when their spirit was hurt for the first time. It was not a fast process. All women in prison wear a series of masks, some of which have been in place for a long time; masks that shield the reality of the lives they have lived not only from other people, but also from themselves. To take off even one of the masks is to risk humiliation and pain, the sort of pain that comes from the exposure of a gaping wound.

The fear of humiliation comes from their sense that what has happened to them has been their fault, somehow they called the abuse they suffered down on themselves through their own actions. To tell the truth will mean confirmation of their belief that it was their fault and they are stupid and worthless human beings who deserved everything that happened to them.

In 'Watea — Pathways to Freedom', we heard from women whose memory of the first time their spirit was hurt was based on an incident or series of incidents that had happened well before their fifth birthday and involved invasion of their body. We heard women describe incident after incident of sexual abuse, often by the men in their mothers' lives.

'I wake up. My stepfather is lying beside me. His fingers are inside me. My mother is asleep on the other side of him. Why won't she wake up? I am thirteen.'

'My father pushes me back on the bed and holds me down with one hand while he undoes his trousers. He then pushes my knees apart and as I hold my eyes shut, he takes away the innocence of a nine-year-old.'

'He tells me to let him do what he wants to do. He tells me no man will want to marry me unless I let him do what he wants. I am ten years old.'

We heard women describe how by the time they were 11 years of age, they had been abused by five different men; all of them part of their circle of family and friends, and all of the sexual abuse of a serious and ongoing nature rather than a one-off case of inappropriate touching. By the time these women were turning 11 years of age, they had begun to wonder just what it was they were doing or what it was they had emblazoned on their foreheads in ink only the abusers could see, that invited the men to commit the abuse.

It wasn't only in 'Watea — Pathways to Freedom' that the stories of the abuse histories of the women emerged. Many came to light in the process of the women coming to terms with their imprisonment and beginning the journey of self-discovery that being in prison gave them the opportunity to undertake. A lingering memory I have is of the life stories of some of the younger women who had begun appearing in greater numbers at the prison gates, women who had not yet reached their twentieth birthday.

As a result of having been at Christchurch Women's for 18 months, I had become used to the inevitability of some women making their way to prison via drug abuse, violence and prostitution and had become inured to the arrival of 21- to 25-year-olds in the institution. I occasionally wondered at the journeys these young people had taken in life in comparison to my own children, who were about the same age and still had the thought 'there but for the grace of God' sitting in a corner of my mind, but such thoughts were soon moved on by the practicalities of managing women, stroppy women, in a custodial environment.

Then I began to notice the increase in the numbers of younger women. In December 1998, Christchurch Women's Prison had a total muster of 98 inmates. Of those 98 women, 20 were under 20 years of age and all 20 of those young women were in prison for a serious violent offence. The policy of the time was that young women under the age of 17 years sentenced to a term of imprisonment were not to be received into a women's prison, but rather were to be placed in a secure CYFS facility while remaining under the jurisdiction of the superintendent of the nearest women's prison. This was a fine idea in theory, but the reality at that time was fast becoming that the young women were almost completely unmanageable in the CYFS facility given their histories and the degree of manipulation they were capable of and the managers of the CYFS facilities were very keen to have the prison take the young women off their hands.

These young women gave the impression of being 10 feet tall and bulletproof. They were obviously no strangers to violence and they had mouths like sewers. They were difficult to like and difficult to manage. But as with the women spoken of earlier, once they had settled into the prison a little and there was time and room for both sides to take a breath, we went behind the scenes and began to build a picture about the life these young women had led prior to their arrival in prison and a level of understanding began to develop about why they presented as they did.

We heard of an 8-year-old child watching her mother kill her father in a drunken brawl in the family lounge on a Saturday night while she and her two younger brothers looked on. We heard of a 14-year-old child being told by her mother, after a childhood of being passed like a parcel from one member of the family to another, that the reason her mother had given her away when she was born was because she should never have been born. As she tells us this, a solitary tear runs down a face that until now has shown no emotion at all regardless of what anyone has said or done to her during her time in prison. We hear of an 11-year-old child who left home on her eleventh birthday because her father had sexually abused her a number of times over the years and always on her birthday and she had decided on that particular day that 'the bastard' wasn't going to do it again. She had told her mother about the abuse, but nothing changed, so she left the family home and joined the other children and teenagers who live in the pipes that run under the streets of Auckland.

When asked if she had supported herself by prostitution when she left home, this young woman simply smiled and nodded. When asked how she knew what to do, she replied nonchalantly 'my cousin showed me', and when challenged that 11 years old was a very young age at which to be having sex with men for money, she replied, with a look that suggested those she was speaking to had no idea of the real world, that 'they're doing it younger now — eight or nine'. This young woman was 19 years old at the time of this conversation. The life she had led since leaving home at 11 can only be guessed at and it is little wonder she is in prison.

As I tell some of the stories the women told me about their personal histories and the events that had led to their arrival in prison, echoing in my head are the words I frequently hear repeated in the media, whenever there is the suggestion that offenders can also be victims. Words to the effect of being sick of the 'abuse excuse', of being sick of hearing the offender did what they did because they weren't breast-fed long enough as a baby. It would be great if the issue were only whether a child was breast-fed long enough, but unfortunately it isn't.

A young woman who leaves home while still a young child; who sleeps each night in the pipes under the streets of Auckland with other young children; who nobody bothers to look for when she begins life on the streets; who at the age of 13 is regularly walking down dark alleys with strangers, letting them do things to her body and doing the things they want her to do to theirs; who uses drugs to try to allay her ever-present fear and loneliness and her sadness that nobody cares enough to look for her.

104

The day comes when she is desperate for money for drugs and she agrees to do a home invasion with her friends. They break into an old man's house and she gets the job of holding the knife at his throat while her friends ransack the house.

As she holds that knife at his throat, it isn't him she is conscious of — she is holding the knife at the throat of everyone in her life who let her down; she is holding the knife at the throat of every 'bastard' she ever walked down a dark alley with, men who willingly and knowingly paid a child for sex. She is a child, an abandoned and damaged child, and for the first time in her life, she is in control. Little wonder that she stands a while and enjoys the moment. Little wonder that she thinks about stabbing him. The miracle in my view occurs when she doesn't give in to the intense feelings of rage she has to have been feeling in that moment about the life she had been born into and doesn't mortally wound him.

The young woman I have just described is not one young woman; she is almost every young woman who appeared at the gates of Christchurch Women's Prison in my latter time there. Damaged and dangerous children nobody cares about, who didn't ask to be born into the life they were given, but who we collectively abandon and then condemn when the chaotic lifestyle they are living leads them to prison, as it was always going to do. I have often wondered about the irony of the clamour for longer and tougher sentences for violent offenders coming from the same community whose members include men who willingly pay these children for sex, having sought them out specifically because they are children.

I referred to these young women earlier as appearing as if they were 10 feet tall and bulletproof. Some of my saddest moments in my role as manager of Christchurch Women's Prison occurred when these belligerent, foul-mouthed would-be adults began to relax into the safety of the prison environment (safe at least in comparison to the world in which they had been living) and we began to see glimpses of the child within. Slowly as they thawed and began to emerge from behind the shields they had constructed to keep themselves safe, they began to lift their eyes and look directly at the person they were speaking to, their usual habit having been to look at the floor whenever they spoke. In the moments when their eyes met mine, I saw clearly for the first time images of the places they had been, the sights they had seen. In their short lives they had seen more than you and I are ever likely to, they had been places no child should ever have to go and while I was not then, nor am I now, willing to excuse them their crimes or forget the terror they had introduced into other people's lives, I began to understand. I began to wish it had been different for them in their journey through childhood.

I have spoken before of my belief that if we are serious in our quest to successfully reintegrate offenders back into the community and reduce the current high rate of re-offending and make our communities safer, it isn't about making prisons more barbaric and treating those in prison worse than they are treated now. What purpose will be served by making the lives of the young women I have just discussed worse? How, in fact, can you make the life of someone who has lived the life they have lived worse? As a society, we abandon them and let them live as forgotten children. And when they offend, as they do their best to survive in the world into which they have been cast, we seek to make sure they suffer further degradation while in prison, with further reminders of their inherent worthlessness.

It's true that not all those in prison have a personal history similar to the young women I have described. It's true that some of the people currently in our prisons have committed cold, calculated violent offences that have robbed a family of a loved one, after having been given every advantage in life. But what is also true, and what I don't see reflected in the media debate about longer and tougher prison sentences, is that a great many of those in prison have exactly the personal history I have described. What I don't see reflected in the debate is any acceptance that we have all played a part in the creation of the soulless monsters who commit the heinous crimes that sicken us all in terms of their viciousness and senselessness. He or she was once the child we allowed to live unsupported and unloved in the streets; was once the child we allowed to suffer extreme abuse at the hands of those who were supposed to love and protect them and who, against the odds, lived long enough to move from guileless victim to guilty monster.

My experience at Christchurch Women's Prison taught me that if you really want to make the lives of those in prison tough, if you really want them to feel and acknowledge the pain they have inflicted on their victims, you don't feed them less and work them harder. Instead, you bring them face-to-face with themselves. In bringing them to prison, a vacuum has been created and the chaos present in their lives before they came to prison has been removed. None of the distractions that have allowed avoidance of the real issues remain. There are no drugs available (or at least on a good day there are significantly less) to keep the memories submerged. It is in the moment that the inmate comes face-to-face with herself or himself that the real pain is felt and the real journey to acknowledgement of what they have done and whom they have hurt can begin. It is in the telling of the stories of their lives that they can begin to understand the journey they have been on and begin to know the pain they have inflicted on others.

If it's pain you want them to feel in order to assuage the grief and anger you suffer as a result of losing a loved one, know that it is in the telling of their stories that the real pain is felt. If you insist they be subjected to ill-treatment and further degradation, you give them something to fight against — and they are well used to fighting. If you allow the creation of a vacuum and leave them with themselves, they have nothing to fight against except themselves.

Storytelling is not the easy option. It is the exposure of a deep and festering wound that has been covered with bandages of varying sorts for many years. The poison has seeped out from time to time and another bandage has been placed across the top of the wound in the hope that this one will be strong enough and absorbent enough to contain the wound within its existing boundaries. The removal of the bandage is a painful exercise of and by itself and what follows is a long, slow, painful healing process. The wound sits exposed and it is through the expression of grief, the crying of tears, that the wound is cleansed and the skin begins to knit together. The first tears are for the life the person was born into, but as their awareness and strength grows, they reach the point of being able to cry for the person or people they hurt in their journey to prison. It is in that profound moment of awareness that the true magic occurs.

I have watched again and again as women who have been given the space to think about themselves and their lives, women who came into prison railing against the unfairness of the world and denying all responsibility for the crime for which they have been convicted, have stood to own the chaos that was their life before prison. They have finally owned their crime and the hurt they have inflicted on others and expressed their resolve to make their own future and the future of their children a more positive experience. I have watched the light come on in the eyes of women as they have realised that they do have a place in the world; they do have a contribution to make; they do have the right to be alive. It was in those moments that my strong belief in women's prisons as one of the major focal points at which we can and should begin to impact real societal change in terms of our high rates of imprisonment, youth suicide and child abuse was born.

'It hurts a little less every time the story is told . . . every time.'

'We all move on from the hurt, the grief in our lives if someone listens to our story.'

It is important to note when considering the idea of storytelling as a mechanism by which offenders come to truly know the hurt they have inflicted on others, that while it was the women in prison who showed me storytelling is a mechanism that can help in putting the pieces of their shattered lives back together, it was also very clear that the women were not seeking forgiveness or pity. Those in the community who claim to be sick of the 'abuse excuse' appear to be focused on the possibility that if credence is given to the abuse suffered by offenders, they will be excused punishment, given a hug and told to go on their way.

This was not the expectation of the women who told their stories to the public of Canterbury at the Watea and Kia Maumahara performances. They were adamant that they neither wanted nor expected the pity or the forgiveness of the audience and were clear in declaring their ownership of their crimes. They were adamant that they had entered the process in order to better understand themselves and the journey they had been on and to come to grips with the impact of their crimes on their victims. They told the stories of their lives to the public in the hope that they would lead to an increased public awareness of the journey to prison and that the telling of their stories would make a difference in the lives of children. For themselves, they accepted that they had committed a crime and they would do the time.

'I own my sentence.'

'A good man died because of me.'

'My daughter died because of me.'

In terms of what they did expect from the members of the public they were in discussion with after the performances, the women asked only that when the time came for their release, they be given adequate support to begin the process of rebuilding their lives. They knew that unless they were supported in their efforts to make a new start, the chances of success were minimal.

The hurdles women face upon release from prison are immense. For many men, the journey out of prison is a simple process that sees them rejoin the life they left behind when they entered. Their wife or partner has continued to maintain the family home, to pay the bills and to raise the children. Within 72 hours many men are living a life identical to the life they were living on the day they were sentenced. For many women, on the other hand, there is nothing to return to.

Her partner has moved on, her children have been placed in care and the possessions she owned at the time she was sentenced have been lost, misplaced or stolen. When that reality is added to the judgement she encounters from the community for being a woman who has been in prison, judgement that seems to hold women to greater account than men for having been a prison inmate, the dreams she dreamed in those moments before she was released come under intense pressure. It isn't long before she begins to dream different dreams; dreams of an injection that will return her to a place where she cannot feel the pain; dreams of a place where she doesn't have so many mountains to climb. Within 72 hours many women have given in to the temptation to reinsert the needle in their arm and have begun the journey back to prison.

7: The connections

New Zealand has one of the highest imprisonment rates in the world, second only to the United States, with over 5000 people currently in our 17 prisons. We could be excused for thinking the problem is huge, too big to handle, and the only realistic option available to us is building more prisons. Recent announcements about new prisons planned and the extensions to be added to the existing ones could lead us to believe that decision has already been made. What I have found interesting, whenever I have paused to consider the extent of the problem and what we as a society might do about it, is the connectedness able to be seen when just who is in prison becomes the focus.

Throughout my time in the male prison service, I noticed there were often a number of members from the same family in prison together. It was interesting to watch the faces of long-serving male officers when it was mentioned in the staff canteen that 'so and so' had been received into the institution the previous evening. The response was often a shrug, and the impression I gained as I watched such exchanges was that in the minds of the officers, the admission of a member of 'that' family into prison was as inevitable as the arrival of dusk at the end of the day.

Unfortunately, there appeared to be a negative aspect to this recognition of certain family names as part of the regular cycling of inmates through the prison system. It allowed many prison staff to rest in the belief that people came to prison because they were a member of a bad family, rather than because their life circumstances might have predisposed them to a life where crime was seen as acceptable behaviour, with occasional prison sentences the inevitable result. This in turn often affected the way in which the inmates were treated and limited the opportunities they were given, while in prison, to seriously consider the option of a crime-free life. It doesn't matter how many programmes a person is offered to learn about managing their anger or living a drug-free life, if every time they look into the face of an officer in the prison in which they are serving their sentence, they see the message that they are from 'that' family and are therefore a 'natural crim'.

The family connections cannot be denied and must be worked with if any progress is to be made. When I arrived at Christchurch Women's Prison, it quickly became apparent that there were strong familial connections among the prison populations in Canterbury.

The closeness of the Canterbury community and the fact that three prisons are located in the area, so local offenders can usually be accommodated at a local institution, meant that the connections were clearly visible. One of the women resident at Christchurch Women's Prison was serving a term of imprisonment with her adult daughter, while members of both her immediate and extended family were in prison over the road at Christchurch Men's Prison. She wasn't unusual; there were a number of other inmates with immediate family resident in the men's prison as well.

As my time at Christchurch Women's Prison extended and I began to learn more about the Canterbury community, it seemed as if there were key families at the heart of almost all the criminal activity in the area. There were new offenders, those who came from previously crime-free families, but they were in the minority. It slowly began to occur to me that if the key families were removed from Canterbury, the crime rate would drop by about 80 per cent, and I decided to attempt to raise the awareness of the community about the inevitability of prison for some children.

When invited to speak about the reality of prison, I began to suggest that if five families were removed from the environs of Canterbury, a significant drop in the crime rate would probably be noticed quite quickly. The reaction I received was interesting.

While I hadn't simply plucked the figure of five families from the air, neither had I stopped to identify the actual families, as I had no desire to be involved in discussion about specific well-known local families. I had made an educated guess based on my knowledge of the families who were known to the longer-serving prison staff. Whenever I spoke publicly about the issue of familial connections within the criminal networks and made my suggestion, the audience would overtly begin to tick the five families off on their fingers and nod their heads in recognition of the truth of what I was saying. It would seem it is a well-recognised fact that there are a small number of families at the centre of the majority of the crime being committed in Christchurch and I am sure it is the same in every community in New Zealand. If asked, I am confident the police could easily identify the familial connections among those committing the majority of the crime within every community. And I don't believe I'm telling anyone something they don't already know.

Having acknowledged this reality, however, it is the next step that is the difficult one. What I watched happening in the male prison environment, the shrugging of the shoulders and the acceptance of the inevitability of a person's arrival in prison because of their family background, also happens regularly in the community. The community knows who the main offenders in their area are, but that knowledge doesn't lead to anything other than an automatic acceptance of the idea of someone being a natural criminal and therefore beyond help. I believe it is this acceptance that has given rise to the idea that by making prisons tougher and less desirable places, by making prison sentences longer, these 'natural criminals' will make the choice to stop offending and lead a crime-free life. If only it were so simple.

Let me take you back to the woman who was in prison with

her daughter while members of both her immediate and her extended family served a term of imprisonment at Christchurch Men's Prison. Her term of imprisonment related to drug offences. She had served other prison sentences for similar offences, each time receiving a longer term of imprisonment because her repeat offending was seen as a sign of her unwillingness to learn the error of her ways. The system considered her to be a criminal by choice rather than by accident. Given her age and her intelligence, it was not a totally off-the-wall suggestion that this woman was choosing a life of crime rather than being a victim of the process. When I first met her, I had the sense of a woman totally in control of her own destiny, a woman totally aware of the consequences of her offending. She was a woman with a very tough exterior and in the initial few months of her sentence, we had a number of discussions about just who was running the prison. At times I actually felt she was, although I was loath to let her know that. But as she settled into her sentence, I had the opportunity to learn about her background and the life she had experienced growing up, and I began to understand the real reasons she was in prison.

In contrast to previous sentences, during this sentence she began to demonstrate a willingness to explore her background with a view to identifying what lay behind her offending. During previous sentences, she had rejected the idea of doing any programmes that targeted her offending patterns. In fact, she had revealed in some of the discussions we had during the time we spent together at Christchurch Women's that on previous occasions the imposition of a prison sentence hadn't slowed up her drug dealing at all, either in the community or in the prison. I believed her.

This time was different. This time she had a grandson, a beautiful baby boy — blond-haired as it happens, but I can't recall his eye colour. While she accepted with reluctance the fact that her daughter's drug addiction had led her to prison and may return her there a number of times before she found the strength to 'clean up', she retained a strong hope that prison was something her grandson would never experience. Deep in her heart I believe she knew the degree to which the odds were stacked against him, but she was clear in her determination that if it were up to her, it wouldn't happen. With his face firmly planted in the forefront of her mind, she began the difficult task of unravelling her past and making the connections to the place in which she now found herself.

Her earliest memory? She is two years old, and as she moves around the kitchen listening to the adults in the room, Dad and Grandad are sitting at the kitchen table. They are dealing drugs. Let's just pause for a moment and consider that scenario. What are children supposed to learn from their grandparents? Grandparents are the providers of the good stuff in life, the ones who, when you're small, seem to love you unconditionally, while your parents are the ones who keep making you eat what's good for you and insist you go to bed before you're tired. In this particular child's life, there is no reason to suppose her grandfather was in any way different to the norm, and yet he dealt drugs for a living. The obvious conclusion this small, impressionable child would reach, once she came to understand a little more about what was involved, had to be that dealing drugs was an OK thing to do. Her grandad did it.

Compare the situation this child was in with another child in another kitchen. This is a kitchen in a house in a more upmarket area of town. As the 2-year-old child moves around the kitchen listening to the adults in the room, Dad and Grandad are sitting at the kitchen table. They're not dealing drugs — they're discussing the enrolment of the child at Christ's College and his entry to Canterbury University. Once he's graduated, they continue to visualise, he'll follow them into the family law firm. It is my belief that in the two scenarios just described, exactly the same thing is happening; a 2-year-old child is learning about the pathways of life that lie in front of them.

It could be said that both children will have a number of

opportunities to reject the pathways they are glimpsing as 2-year-olds, before they decide on the direction they will take in life. But what I think it is important to focus on here, as we consider the idea of people being 'natural criminals' and coming from 'naturally bad' families, is the difficulty involved when the path in life we might want to take is completely outside the value system or realm of experience of those we love and respect.

Featured on the front page of the *Dominion* newspaper a year or so ago, under the headline 'Family Tradition' was an article concerning the swearing in of a new High Court judge. In the accompanying photograph, the Justice is posing with his young daughter, who is wearing the wig that is part of the attire her father will wear as a High Court judge. The article explains that the little girl's grandfather was also a High Court judge.

On a page inside the same *Dominion* newspaper, was the story and accompanying photograph of two brothers who had punched and kicked to death a 41-year-old father of six in Wanganui's main street in June 2000. The two brothers were sentenced to terms of six years and three-and-a-half years imprisonment for the offence. The caption that ran under the photograph of the two men as they stepped from a police van was 'Michael, left, and Kelvin Kumeroa . . . victims of a violent and abusive upbringing.' In the article it was reported that Kelvin Kumeroa had said in admitting his part in the beating: 'No one beats up my brother and gets away with it.' In sentencing the two men, Justice Ellis said that probation and psychiatric reports showed the brothers to be victims of a violent and abusive upbringing, and that Kelvin in particular must be offered a chance to learn to control his anger.

As I compared the two stories, it seemed to me that both could have been headed with the words that sat above the photo of the Justice and his daughter — 'Family Tradition'. They are both family traditions; one a family tradition of study of the law and a commitment to public service; the other a family tradition of violence and loyalty to family when a member of the family is threatened. Certainly they are very different family traditions, but the extent to which they are traditions, and as such, have a strong hold on the members of the family, needs to be understood if we are going to have any chance of addressing the levels of violence, abuse and crime that exist in our society.

Let's return to the woman who was in prison with her daughter while members of both her immediate and her extended family served a term of imprisonment at Christchurch Men's Prison. When she was in her early teens, her mother was serving a term of imprisonment at Christchurch Women's Prison.

She is able to describe vividly, and with a great deal of humour, how at various times during her mother's term of imprisonment she was involved in smuggling illicit goods into prison for her mother. On one occasion she and some friends cut a hole in the fence that surrounded the prison and ran remote-control cars up to the windows of the minimum-security wing. The amusing aspect of this story is that whereas today any attempt to smuggle contraband into a prison would inevitably involve drugs, that wasn't what was taped to the top of the remote-control cars. The goods being smuggled in were bacon and paua.

On another occasion she was apparently involved in a smuggling exercise that saw her mother's partner, her mother's best friend's partner and a 'spare' man enter the prison for a brief time. (I feel the need to reinforce here that this was some years ago — institution security was obviously less stringent than it is today!) The description she gave of the way in which the men gained entry to the prison and the degree of exhaustion exhibited by the 'spare' man after the exercise (so to speak) was really very funny.

The point of my repeating these stories is neither to poke fun at the security of the institution nor to downplay the seriousness of smuggling illicit goods, or men, into a prison. The point I am seeking to reinforce is the degree to which children's views of the world are influenced by the world in which they live.

As she took part in her father's swearing-in ceremony, the

Justice's young daughter was learning about a world that involves public service, commitment to excellence and family tradition. As a teenager, the woman serving a term of imprisonment for drug offences took part in an exercise involving smuggling illicit goods in to her mother in prison. She was learning about a world that involves getting the breaks where you can, being clever in what you do and family tradition.

It isn't about excusing crime or minimising the effect of crime on its victims. In trying to come to terms with the complexity of the issues behind our high imprisonment and re-offending rates and the increasing levels of violence manifesting within our communities, it seems to me the starting point is the recognition and acceptance of the reality demonstrated by these stories. Not all children in this country start their lives in the same place. Once we recognise and accept this, it seems to me we will be in a better position to know where and how to make the difference that will matter. In the words of one male inmate: 'I am third generation Black Power. I have been Black Power all my life; it's all I know. It's been bred into me to be a violent person. I learned violence from my grandparents.'

Throughout the time I spent working in prisons, I was constantly confronted with the realisation that almost everyone has dreams. It is only in the content of their dreams that human beings differ from one another. Occasionally I found myself in the presence of someone who no longer dared to dream, but fortunately those moments were few and far between. It was a sad experience, but I felt a greater sadness when I realised exactly what dreams some of those who had found their way into prison had based their actions and their belief about life on as they began their journey.

As a teenager testing the waters of adulthood, my son found himself experiencing a few hours locked in a cell in a local police station because he spat in the direction of a police officer. ('I wasn't spitting *at* him, Mum, just in his general direction!') He was not only upset by the experience, he was also angry. He knew he didn't belong in a police cell and while he was fully aware of the sequence of events that had landed him in his predicament, he had enough belief in himself to know the experience wasn't an indicator of things to come. As he sat in that cell waiting for his mother — and the lecture that would inevitably accompany her — he held on to the idea he didn't belong there. His experience was in stark contrast to many of the people I have met in prison.

When some of our young offenders wake up in a police cell having been 'out of it' on drugs for most of the previous 12 hours, when they stand in the dock of a courtroom and hear the judge deliver a sentence of imprisonment, unlike my son, they feel no anger. In fact, they often feel nothing at all except a sense that the world is exactly as they expect it to be. In the moment when they wake up in the police cell, their dream has just come true. From the time they were very young children, many of them have lived either in a world where prison was something to be endured, a facet of life all adults in their world experienced, or in a world that reminded them regularly of their worthlessness and the inevitability of prison as a destination.

With regard to the idea of connectedness, I have spoken to date only about the children of families whose behaviour and attitudes predispose their children to prison. The obvious response to the idea that Michael and Kelvin Kumeroa were victims of a violent and abusive upbringing, as reported when they were sentenced to terms of imprisonment for punching and kicking a man to death, is to look towards the parents or the caregivers who had responsibility for these two men when they were growing up.

I have no knowledge at all of these men or the circumstances in which they were raised, beyond what was reported in the newspaper, but it is natural to wonder who didn't do their job, who allowed these men to be abused as children. In my opinion, whoever allowed the boys to be subject and witness to violence as they were growing up were in effect standing with these men when they punched and kicked a man to death.

119

But while I am clear about the connections between the childhood the boys experienced and the crime of violence the men committed, this is the point at which the picture begins to blur for me, the point at which the world of black and white, of right and wrong, begins to take on a greyish hue. I am no longer certain who can ultimately be held accountable for the violent deeds being committed on our streets and in our homes. I know the person standing in front of me is the one who did the burglary, the one who robbed the service station or the one who stabbed the old man, but I also know that it goes beyond the issue of parents or caregivers in terms of who plays a part in the commission of a violent act.

There is the issue of abused and damaged children surviving an abusive childhood and in time becoming the abusers, as in the case of the Kumeroa brothers. At the same time, there is also the issue of parents having no choice but to induct their children into the world of crime because there appear to be no other means of survival. And ultimately, there is the issue of it mattering where you live in this country and what chance you get to succeed in life when you are considered to be from a 'bad' family and a 'natural criminal'.

When I entered the prison service in 1985, it seemed as if the male inmates themselves decided when they would stop coming to prison. The majority appeared to come, as I have said, as part of their journey to manhood and almost accidentally. Many came back a number of times before they were willing to believe that no matter how clever they thought they were being in doing whatever it was they were doing that was illegal, the chances were fairly high that they would be caught and receive another prison sentence. As a degree of maturity worked its way into their lives (very slowly for some), they would begin to realise the futility of prison and to admit to themselves how tired they were of forever being told by people in green uniforms what to do. It was generally in that moment they began to think about other ways of living. Programmes were offered to inmates, programmes aimed at addressing the issues lying behind their offending, but my sense was that it was often only when he fell in love or when his partner had a child, that an inmate would make the decision not to return to prison.

With all due respect to the programme staff working in prisons at the time, it seemed to be almost in spite of what they were being offered in prison rather than because of it, that some men stopped coming. When the inmate made the decision to complete the sentence he was serving and not return, he left prison and within a day or two was employed as a labourer on a building site and the justice system never saw him again. The problem today, or at least one of them, is that there are no jobs as labourers on building sites waiting for the men, or women, who come out of prison.

I am not an economist and my daughter, who has a degree in economics, will happily tell you that while her mother has a good grasp of social justice issues, she struggles to understand economic policy. But what I do know, and can speak about from experience, is that in the years since I began working in the area of social justice, New Zealand society has become a much harder place in which to survive. The gap between rich and poor has widened to a chasm and we now have both third-generation unemployed and third-generation prison inmates.

In fact, when I spoke about this issue recently to a group of school principals, one of them put up his hand and corrected me. He said for him it was now fourth generation — he had just enrolled a child whose great-grandfather had been a pupil at the school. None of the adults in the family were in employment and all the male adults in the family had served a term of imprisonment. In his view the outlook for the child wasn't good. I agree.

Let me be clear. I am not suggesting poverty or lack of advantage justifies criminal behaviour. As I am constantly hearing quoted in the media, there are many poor families in society who live law-abiding lives and poverty doesn't have to equal crime. But in dismissing the link between financial hardship and crime, we run the risk of being a little too sanctimonious about what it is to live close to or beneath the breadline. As the potential link between poverty and crime has been debated in the media, it has often occurred to me that the people who dismiss any link often do so from a position of relative wealth. They have no idea about what it's like to live hand-to-mouth, to see no hope of changing that way of life on the horizon and to want better for your children. It seems that as the gap between rich and poor has widened in our society, so too has the arrogance of the 'rich' grown in terms of the views they hold about how everyone else should live.

Everyone wants a good life for their children. In a society where the bottom rungs of the ladder leading to a fulfilled life have been removed through economic reform, it isn't surprising that we now have to deal with the reality of career criminals. When those returning to their lives in urban centres after serving a term of imprisonment can't find a job that will allow them to earn enough to live while they begin to grapple with the changes in their lives that are necessary to keep them out of prison, it's little wonder they choose to continue their involvement in criminal activity. From their perspective there are few other options and it then becomes a case of learning to play the odds, knowing that the occasional prison sentence will be the inevitable consequence of their choice. And so the cycle continues.

And then there is the issue of where you live and how the world greets you when it knows you live in 'that' part of town, when you are a member of 'that' family. As I said at the beginning of this chapter, it really doesn't matter how many programmes an inmate is offered to learn about managing their anger or living a drug-free life, if every time they look into the face of a prison officer they see themselves written off as a 'natural crim', because of their family name. And it isn't just about the interactions between inmates and prison officers; it's also about the look the child sees in the eyes of almost every person in a position of authority they meet, when they say where they live or who their parents are. It's about the sense the child develops from a very early age that they're not like the rest, they're not 'normal' and should have no expectations the world will treat them well or offer them opportunities to succeed.

I have met young men and women who, in the midst of a life of total chaos, can remember the one teacher in their entire school career who appeared to believe in them; the one foster mum out of the 20 foster mothers they had who seemed to really care; the brief interaction with an adult that left them with the idea that they did have something unique to contribute to the world. These same young men and women can describe with heart-wrenching clarity the look they have seen in people's eyes most of their lives, a look that consigns them to the scrapheap of life. It was a sobering thought to realise that the people they were talking about when they described this 'look' weren't the adults in the immediate circle of their lives, but you and I. It seems we play a significant role in determining the degree to which these children believe in themselves and are often the ones who ensure they never reach their potential, never have a dream beyond entry to prison.

In his column published in the *Sunday Star Times* on 16 December 2001, Michael Laws wrote:

Hundred of thousands of underprivileged New Zealanders come from underprivileged backgrounds. Hundreds of thousands of New Zealanders come from broken homes, were the victims of domestic violence, suffered sexual and emotional abuse. And yet most lead decent lives. They try to raise their kids to lead better lives than theirs and be gifted opportunities that were denied their youth.

I agree that many people have successfully overcome difficult backgrounds and succeeded in giving their children a much better life than the one they endured as children, often because at a critical stage in their life they met someone who invested them with a sense of self that carried them beyond the degradation and deprivation of their childhood.

What I cannot accept is when he goes on to say: 'The mass of the criminal class are recidivist offenders. They are incorrigible.' In my experience with 15 years of mixing with the so-called criminal class, I can assure you 'the mass of them' are not incorrigible; they are anything but, in fact. They are resilient people whom life has continued to dump on from a great height while the rest of us watch, who refuse to give in to their lingering sense of having no right to be here with us, the people they see as 'normal'. They are people whose courage and determination to continue to make the best of the place in which they find themselves far exceeds anything I have seen exhibited by those born to more privileged lives. And they are people who constantly remind me of the magic of this thing we call life. It can't be denied that there are some who fit the description of 'incorrigible', but we would all do well to realise they make up perhaps 5 per cent, maybe even less, of the current prison population.

Whatever mistakes I made as I raised my children (and there were many), I can rest in the knowledge they know they are special and have a contribution to make to the world, and that for me they come first, now and forever. In deciding what to do about the increasing crime and violence in our society and before we come to believe as a society that more prisons, longer sentences and tougher prison conditions are the answer, I think it a good idea for us to pause. We should take some time to think about the children who have never known they are special, who have never known the experience of someone putting them first. Before we tell ourselves such children are the sole concern of those who bore them, I think we need to reflect at least a little on the reality that we all play a part, albeit a small one, in the condemnation of many of these children to a life of crime. And so we all play a part in the pain and hurt suffered by victims of crime in our communities.

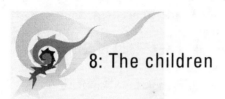

8: The children

As I prepare to send this manuscript to the publisher, the news has just broken of three young women, children in fact, being charged for the part they allegedly played in the death of a 60-year-old man in Waitara. The young women are all aged 14 years. Two have been charged with the man's murder, the third with being an accessory after the fact. A 13-year-old boy has also been arrested for being an accessory after the fact. Due to his age he will be dealt with by Police Youth Aid. In the story that ran on the front page of the *Dominion* on 16 February 2002 about the arrest of these young people, mention was made of the fact that the police investigation into the death of the man had focused on 'a group of Waitara street kids who wander the streets late into the night'. As I read the story, I couldn't help but wonder if any of the young people involved in the murder were among the group of students I spoke to late last year, when I visited Waitara High School.

I had arranged to visit the school as part of the work I was undertaking for Specialist Education Services in the aftermath of the furore about the blond, blue-eyed 5-year-old. In the course of my visit, and at the request of the school, I spent some time with a group of students who were considered to be at risk. They were kids who were perceived to be living on the edge; whose futures were uncertain for a whole range of reasons that centered on a lack of stability in their lives. My role in talking to these students was to try to focus them at least a little on the reality of prison and to reinforce that whatever might be happening in their lives, however difficult or unfair their lives had been through no fault of their own until this point, ultimately they, and only they, would make the choice to go to prison. I guaranteed that whatever they had heard or seen about prison, however easy they had been told it was to do a prison sentence, I was sure they wouldn't like it if they ever made it there. Perhaps now, a mere four months later, some of them have.

The group of students I spoke to weren't bad kids. Some of them wore a tough exterior and I had to be quite blunt on occasion to get across the reality of prison. A number of them had been told prison was easy, a prison sentence was no big deal. But as I continued to describe some of the things that could happen to them in prison that prison officers are unable to prevent, they began to appear less relaxed about prison as a destination.

Despite the tough exteriors and the bad language (intended to show me I was dealing with adults and not a bunch of children), it was possible to see these young people each had their dreams and were hopeful about what they might achieve in life. Despite the fact life hadn't been good to most of them so far, they were still able to believe good things can happen and they might be one of the lucky ones. It was also possible to see life had definitely not been good to the majority of them. They hadn't spent much of their childhood indulging in innocent laughter. The shields they wore against the world that translated into difficult behaviour in the school environment were there because of the pain and hurt they had suffered. And as I thought about them after our discussion, I wondered for how many of them it was already too late. How many of them were, due to the neglect and abuse in their lives, already on the path that would see a senseless violent act committed and their dreams shattered, to be replaced by a prison cell?

As I think about those young people now, I also think about two men, one of whom I knew personally, albeit briefly, and the other whom I know only through the media. The first of these

126

men is Dean Hiroki, a man whose tattooed face featured in the media when he pleaded guilty to nine charges relating to an attack in which a woman was raped at knifepoint in Wellington, charges for which he was sentenced to preventative detention. The particularly horrifying aspect of his offending was that he took a 14-year-old boy who had been placed in his care by CYF with him when he went out to commit the rape. An article in the July 2000 edition of *North and South* magazine, written by journalist Lauren Quaintance, attempts to convey the horror experienced by the victim in the 15-minute ordeal and leaves the reader with a sense of a life if not permanently ruined, at least severely damaged.

There is no excuse for Dean Hiroki's behaviour and I would not attempt to offer one. But as I look at the dead eyes looking back at the world in the photo on the front page of the *Dominion* after he pleaded guilty to the offences, I remember the 16-year-old boy who sat in my office when I was his probation officer. I also remember visiting him in a police cell the morning after he was arrested for breaking into a house and attempting to sexually violate a woman, late in 1984. He hadn't long begun his association with the Mongrel Mob and I can remember him talking about the sense of belonging and acceptance being in the gang gave him. As I look at the face of the 31-year-old man, I remember that 16-year-old boy and wonder where he has gone and at what particular moment he left. Wherever it is he went, we can be sure it's to a place from which he will never return.

Without doubt, it is too late for Dean, he has inflicted too much hurt on too many people. As I look again at the photo, I wonder how many young people are currently standing on the edge of the same precipice he stood on at 16 and which, if they step off, will lead to them committing a serious crime and being lost to us forever.

The second of the men is Taffy Hotene, a man known to all of New Zealand for the brutal way in which he murdered 22-year-old Kylie Jones. The sentencing judge described the attack as 'savage, barbarous, brutal, ferocious and sadistic'. There are no words to adequately describe the horror of what Kylie must have gone through in those final hours, nor to describe the pain her family and friends have suffered and will go on suffering in the aftermath of her death. As I think about Kylie and the tragedy of her life and the lives of other young women being cut short, I think also of Taffy and wonder what made him the man (some would say monster) he is. My desire to understand more of the man is motivated not by a desire to find an excuse for his behaviour, but rather by a desire to ensure we do what we can to prevent any more young women dying in the way Kylie did.

In an article that appeared in the *Dominion* newspaper on the day after Taffy was sentenced to life imprisonment with a minimum non-parole period of 18 years, his lawyer expressed the view that Taffy had a brutal upbringing in foster care after being abandoned by his mother at three months of age. 'By age 14 his die was cast. He killed kittens, was cruel to other children and hostile to women.' It seems to me that if we are going to prevent the violent deaths of other young women and make our communities safer places for our children and grandchildren, ensuring Taffy Hotene stays in prison for as long as necessary, perhaps for the term of his natural life, is an important but secondary issue. The primary issue has to be getting to the children at risk before their die is cast in order to prevent further unnecessary deaths. No matter how long Taffy is held in prison, nor for that matter how badly he is treated, Kylie Jones will never return to her family, will never turn 25 or 40, will never give her parents grandchildren. That reality has to remain our focus.

In recent times, there have been numerous examples reported in the media of serious violent offending by young people barely into their teens.

The story that ran in the *Dominion* on 16 March 2002 I have already referred to was headlined 'Teens held for deaths of two men' and featured the story of the arrests made following the death of the man in Waitara, and the appearance in the Youth

128

Court in Wellington of two boys aged 16 and 17 years who had been charged with causing grievous bodily harm after a 68-year-old man was found dead in his flat in a Wellington suburb.

Among the clippings I have kept from newspapers since I began to consider the possibility of writing this book are the following.

- *Dominion* 17 February 2000
A 15-year-old girl has begun a life sentence for the frenzied killing of a middle-aged man, making her possibly the young-est female to be convicted of murder in New Zealand.

This young woman was just 12 days past her fifteenth birthday when she repeatedly stabbed 59-year-old Raymond Mullins with a steak knife. At the time of the offence she was reported to have a string of serious offences to her name and was on bail for aggravated robbery. Her 20-year-old sister and an 18-year-old friend were also convicted of murder for their part in the killing.

In an article that appeared in the *New Zealand Herald* under the heading 'A natural born killer at 15' in the days following the sentencing of this young woman, the statement was made that:

—— *was never going to be a typical teenager. Sexually abused as a child, a primary school dropout, prostitute and drug user at 11, armed robber at 13 — it was no surprise to police when she graduated to murder.*

She herself said to police just days after the murder: 'I was just hard-out stabbing him. I felt evil. The place went cold like a freezer, and I knew I had killed him.'

- *Dominion* March 2001
A 14-year-old schoolboy was jailed yesterday for his part in an attack last October that left Levin teenager Ben Oxnam

with his skull fractured from ear to ear. Ben had been punched
and kicked by the 14-year-old and a 13-year-old boy who was
too young to be charged. The 13-year-old had reportedly told
police he attacked Ben because: 'It's what you do. If you want
something you take it.'

• *Dominion* 18 July 2001
A 14-year-old girl has been jailed for three years on charges of
sexual violation, attempted rape, robbery and kidnapping.

The girl was sentenced in Tauranga District Court because
the charges were too serious for the Youth Court. The offences
were committed against two 13-year-olds, a girl and a boy. The
14-year-old girl was in the company of an 18-year-old, a 16-
year-old, a 13-year-old and an 11-year-old when the offences
were committed, but she had been the main offender.

She was just short of her fourteenth birthday when she committed the offences and had, according to her lawyer, been failed
by every social welfare system and her own family. She had
dropped out of school at age 12.

In an article that appeared the following day in the *Dominion*, it was identified that the youngest offenders locked up in
New Zealand's prisons were now girls. The article repeated the
story of the girl mentioned above and reported that the previous
week another 14-year-old girl had been sentenced to four and a
half years' imprisonment for aggravated robbery and home invasion. She too had been sent from the Youth Court to the District
Court because of the seriousness of the crimes. At the time this
article was written, the Department of Corrections had custody
of these two 14-year-old girls together with two 15-year-olds
(both male), fifteen 16-year-olds (all male) and fifty-six 17-year-
olds, of whom fifty-one were male.

In an article written by a *Dominion* journalist in the week
following the sentencing of the 14-year-old girl in the Tauranga
District Court to three years' imprisonment, it was identified

that the girl had been 'born to a Mt Maunganui 15-year-old.' The principal of the intermediate school she attended briefly described her as 'one of those poor little souls who don't get enough love' and noted that she was not a serious truant, but had gone missing from school a couple of times towards the end of her form two year. She never went to secondary school.

- *Dominion* 18 September 2001
A 14-year-old boy with a mental age of eight stood in the dock at Wellington District Court yesterday as an adult and was sentenced to two and a half years' jail for home invasion and aggravated robbery.

The court was told he helped attack three elderly women so his female co-offender, aged 14, 'would like him'.

He had apparently been neglected all his life and had been visited by family only once during the five months he had been on remand in a young offenders' centre. He was described by his lawyer as 'very much the victim of what has been a deprived and tragic background'. As she left the court following his sentencing, his lawyer observed that if things had been put in place for her client, 'things could have been very different than they are now'.

- *Dominion* 18 September 2001
Gasps of shock greeted the appearance of a sobbing 12-year-old boy in Papakura Youth Court yesterday, one of nine young people charged over the robbery and death of pizza deliverer Michael Choy.

The article notes that lawyers at their desks in the court and members of the victim's family were all shocked at how small, slight and young the boy looked. In response to questions from the judge, the boy's lawyer said the boy had not been in school for about two years. The others charged in connection with the robbery and murder of 40-year-old Michael Choy included a boy aged 14, three boys aged 15, a boy aged 16, a young woman who had turned 17 on the day of the crime and two 20-year-old women.

They are shocking stories, shocking in the amount and intensity of violence involved in the offending and made all the more shocking by the age of those involved. The age of the offenders does not in any way excuse them from the incalculable damage that has been done both to their victims and to the families and friends of the victims. It is entirely appropriate that they be punished, that their freedom to live among us be removed for a time. As I think about each of those young people spending time in prison, I can only hope that, as I have said previously, they are given the opportunity to come face-to-face with themselves while they are there, because it will only be in the moment of coming face-to-face with themselves that the journey to a genuine acknowledgement of what they have done and the pain they have inflicted on others can begin.

Knowing that their freedom has been curtailed for a time doesn't answer all the questions. Obviously there is the question of how long their freedom has been curtailed for and whether the period imposed is long enough. This is a question that has been an endless source of debate in the media in recent years and one that will no doubt continue to be widely debated.

There is also the question of the impact of the offending on the victims. As I consider the stories outlined above and note the unnecessary and violent deaths, and the trauma suffered by those lucky enough not to be killed in the commission of the offences, I wonder what might have been done to prevent the crimes happening in the first place. In the case of the 14-year-old boy with the mental age of eight, an 82-year-old, wheelchair-bound woman was terrorised in her own home after she left her door open for the district nurse. Another elderly woman was held at knifepoint while her house was searched, and a 69-year-old woman was assaulted and robbed and as a result of the attack, sustained cuts to the head and had a tooth driven up into her gum.

The judge commented at sentencing that in terms of the impact of the offending on the victims, the offenders had essentially 'shattered their belief that they were safe in their homes'. One woman had moved into a rest home as a direct result of the crime.

While we must continue as a society to work to ensure offenders committing crimes such as these are caught and detained, surely we must also work to increase our understanding of the circumstances that surround the commission of the offences. Only when we understand exactly what happened and why, and begin to take some responsibility as a society for the place in which we now find ourselves, can we even begin to seriously grapple with the steps that must be taken. Eight serious crimes including three murders, 27 offenders none of whom are older than 20, and 22 of those 27 no older than 16 — we have a problem. Rather than simply describing a 15-year-old girl as a natural-born killer, we have to take stock of what in our society has led to a child being angry enough to stab a man 19 times and carve an initial into his chest.

In speaking about the 15-year-old girl described in the *New Zealand Herald* as a natural-born killer, Detective Senior Sergeant Dayle Candy suggested it would be wrong to blame the girl's actions entirely on her background. She suggested instead that the girl was a career criminal who 'was climbing the ladder', a girl who 'had a thirst for violence and needed to see how far she could go. I think she was always going to kill someone at some stage . . . It was a challenge to her.'

This was a child who, nobody seems to dispute, was a prostitute at 11 years of age, who was, to quote the *New Zealand Herald* again, 'part of the Otahuhu sex worker scene, hanging out with young girls and transsexuals selling their bodies to make money for drugs and alcohol'. At the same age young girls lucky enough to have been born into a more stable family situation are graduating from dolls to pop stars, this child was regularly having sex with strangers for money — adult men who no doubt sought her out precisely because she was a child. She had continued to live that lifestyle for a number of years, unchallenged by anyone.

We can be horrified at the viciousness of the crime she committed, but I don't believe we have the right to be surprised when she was finally overtaken by the anger that has to have been brewing for some time about her lot in life, and killed someone. And I don't believe we have the right to make ourselves feel better by simply classifying her actions as those of a natural-born killer who was 'always going to kill someone at some stage'.

In speaking about the 14-year-old girl sentenced in Tauranga District Court to three years imprisonment on charges of sexual violation, attempted rape, robbery and kidnapping, Te Puke detective Alan Kingsbury is reported to have taken issue with the views expressed by the principal of the intermediate school the girl attended and the girl's lawyer, both of whom suggested she was 'also a victim, her criminal behaviour a by-product of an unenviable childhood'. He disputed that the girl was as much a victim as anyone else, stating that '[from] the limited dealings I had with her, she didn't show a lot of remorse and was fairly confident'.

This was, by all accounts, a very damaged child, a child whom the system had 'lost' for over two years. I don't know this particular child, but I know many like her and I would suggest that what Detective Kingsbury encountered in his 'limited dealings' with her were bravado and defensiveness against a system that had done nothing but dump on the child for the duration of her short life. The remorse shown by children such as this young girl doesn't look like the remorse exhibited by most adults when they are prepared to admit their wrongdoings and I'm not sure how many adults dealing with damaged children, especially those in positions of authority, know it when they see it.

There can be no doubt that poverty, family instability and the resulting intergenerational abuse and neglect are among the reasons we are seeing an increasing amount of violence in our communities. And if the cases outlined above and what I observed in my final year at Christchurch Women's Prison are anything to go by, it would seem the age of those committing violent offences is continuing to drop. It was my sense of this, my sense that for many children in our communities the path to prison is rapidly shortening, that led me to make the statement about the hypothetical 5-year-old on his way to prison.

I had left Christchurch Women's Prison in September 1999 deeply concerned about the number of damaged children in adults' bodies who were arriving at the gates of the prison before their lives had even really got underway. Some of these children were as young as 15, while a significant number had yet to celebrate their eighteenth birthday.

As I looked at some of the children who were causing concern in classrooms when I took up the contract with Specialist Education Services in mid-2000, I knew with absolute certainty that I had glimpsed their futures in the lives of the damaged young people I had just left at Christchurch Women's Prison. If we pause to remember the 12-year-old-boy who stood in the dock charged with murder, we know there are children who cannot even be guaranteed the years between 5 and 15 as a time within which they can grow up safely, explore their dreams and begin to know what it is they really want from life before something happens to catapult them into a prison cell.

When I spoke with some of the young people resident at Christchurch Women's Prison during my time there, I was often struck by the early age at which they had disconnected from the school system and found myself wondering (in what I now recognise as naiveté) how that was possible. How was it that their absence from school wasn't noticed and acted upon? In reviewing the circumstances of the young people I have discussed here, there seems to be a common factor relating to this very issue.

'A primary school drop-out.'

'She had dropped out of school at age 12.'

'In response to questions from the judge, the boy's lawyer said that the boy had not been in school for about two years.'

It occurs to me now, as it has occurred to me before, that while we tend to focus our attention on families when we look for a place to lay the blame when a crime is committed, perhaps we aren't recognising the degree to which schools play a part in determining the paths taken by children.

In the December 1999 edition of *Metro* magazine, journalist Geraldine Jones told the story of Luke and Mark Reihana, two brothers who, when 15 and 16 years of age respectively, played a part in the murder of Beverley Bouma. They were subsequently convicted of manslaughter.

When I first read the story, I can remember being affected not only by the callous manner in which Beverley Bouma had been killed and the part these two young men had played, but also by the way in which the lives of the boys' parents had been irrevocably changed.

> *The future is uncertain for their parents, save for the fact that not only have they lost their boys, but also their life as they knew it. They have no money; they have sold what few posses-sions they had. They are no longer welcome in Kaingaroa Village . . . Reporoa is equally inhospitable. And Rotorua, which would offer the greatest opportunity, is also too close for comfort.*

As the article portrayed them, these were not uncaring parents who were uninvolved in the lives of their sons. They were hardworking people 'who had been married for 24 years and who had never lived apart while they raised their five children'. The article notes how well mannered the boys appeared and also noted that there 'is a harmony in this home that could not be turned on for the sake of a casual visitor'. This was during an interview conducted at the home of one of the boys' sisters.

As I tried to understand what had led boys such as these into a situation where they had become part of a cruel and unnecessary murder, I was struck by the comment made by the boys' mother as she outlined the attempts she had made to keep her sons involved in the education system following their suspension from Reporoa College for fighting. (Luke had got into a fight, Mark had stood by his brother.)

In addition to the personal responsibility she feels for her boys' actions, she believes that if they hadn't got lost in the education system, they would not be where they are now.

There will be some who will consider that a big 'if', but in my experience and given the degree to which the children I have mentioned above have obviously been alienated from the education system, it is an 'if' to which I am willing to give some credence.

When thinking about children who are not given a decent chance in life, it isn't long before my mind moves to the many abused children in our communities who do not survive, who don't live long enough to strike back at the world in the way some of the children I have talked about have. In an article that appeared in the *Dominion* newspaper on 24 May 2001, Rosemary McLeod told us that statistics revealed the previous week 'showed that 87 children under 14 were killed in this country between 1990 and 1999, mostly by family, extended family or caregivers'. She went on to say that police statistics from 1994 to 2000 'show nearly 20,000 children (19,501) were known to have been the victims of sexual abuse, violence or neglect during that time'. They are horrifying statistics by anybody's standards.

What I have found it interesting to note is that each time the debate about child abuse has raged in the aftermath of yet another incident in which a small child is severely beaten or killed by someone charged with their protection, we don't seem willing or able to make a connection to the wider issue involved.

On some occasions, I grant you, it is hard to see the abused child in the faces of the adults charged with, for example, putting 300 bruises on the body of a 3-year-old boy who died from his injuries. But in my experience, that abused child is almost always there, looking back at the world from within the shell of the body of the adult he or she has grown into. I have always loved the statement made regularly by Jim Moriarty during the Kia Maumahara and Watea productions at Christchurch Women's Prison: 'Everyone is born pure — it is what happens to them afterwards that damages them.'

To recognise the abused child within the abusing adult is not to excuse their behaviour or to forgive them for the death of the child they were supposed to be looking after. Nothing can excuse a child dying in that way. But it will only be in the full recognition and acceptance of the cycle of violence that is being perpetuated within our communities that we, as a society, can hope to find the answers and stop children being beaten to death. Finding someone to blame, someone to hate, each time we learn of a child being beaten or killed might make us feel better, even a little holier-than-thou as we think about the fact that the worst we have ever done to our own children is paddle their bottoms with a hairbrush, but it does little or nothing to address the real issues sitting at the core of the violent behaviour.

It is an unpleasant thought, but as I have looked at the innocent faces of some of the children beaten to death in recent times, I have wondered what their destiny might have been if they had survived. Would they have transformed into an abuser? Would they in time have stood in the dock of a court as a 15-year-old charged with murder as a result of a home invasion that went wrong; as a 25-year-old charged with the death of a child; or, as a 30-year-old charged with the savage beating, rape and murder of a young woman? It seems to me it is entirely possible. As hard as it might be to visualise when you see him now, I believe Taffy Hotene was once a small boy with an innocent face who was full of energy and excitement about the wonder of the world. He was once a child who contained magic, as all children do.

There were moments during my time in the prison service when an incredible sense of sadness would wash over me as I felt, just for a moment, the reality of the life that had been led by the person standing in front of me: the 15-year-old boy describing how out of the 25 foster homes he had been in since he was 8, there had only been one foster mother who seemed to care; the 19-year-old girl describing the moment when her mother told her she should never have been born; the 16-year-old girl worried about the two younger brothers she had left behind when she came to prison, telling me she had written to her alcoholic mother to suggest that if her mother 'would give up the piss, I would give up the dak' (marijuana). I have continued to experience such moments as I have continued my work among at-risk children and families.

One such moment came when I read an article that appeared in the *Nelson Mail* on 24 January 2001 entitled 'The Price of Silence' by journalist Mary Longmore. The article was based on an interview of Te Rangi Whakaruru, the mother of James Whakaruru, who was speaking out for the first time about her son's death and the part she had played in it. The story has all the components I would expect it to have. A child who had a child; a young woman who, after her partner returned to the family home after serving a term of imprisonment for beating her son, fought her mother for custody because she 'didn't want her son growing up knowing she had given him away, as her parents had done with her'; a family that 'had lived with child abuse for generations'. As I read Te Rangi's account of how she had left her son on the night he died to go to the home of the mother of her partner, the man who was beating her son to death, to get some potatoes, I understood that it hadn't been potatoes she was seeking but help — help for the little boy she loved and help for herself as she struggled to find a way to make it all stop. But when she arrived at the house, 'the words just wouldn't come out'.

As I think about Te Rangi and her inability to say the words: 'He is killing my boy', I accept that we as a society couldn't have done anything to save James at that point. I understand the paralysis that stopped Te Rangi from saying anything to her partner's mother or stopping at her family's home or the police station, both of which she passed on her journey that night. But I also accept a share of the responsibility for James' death, as I believe we all must. In the words of her uncle, Rangi Whakaruru, in an article published in the *New Zealand Herald* on 1 July 2000:

> *The real tragedy aside from the act of murder, lay in the assumption that a young, vulnerable, impressionable teenager who was doing her best to survive in an abusive relationship could protect another more vulnerable life besides her own.*

In my view it is an assumption we all made and one we continue to make from the safety of our living rooms.

In an interview on television around the time Mark Middleton threatened to kill Paul Dally, the man convicted of beating, raping and murdering his stepdaughter, Karla Cardno, if he is ever released from prison, Middleton stated that the reason he made the threat was because 'we care about our children'. Anyone who knows me and the views I hold about longer sentences, tougher sentences, harsher prison conditions and the possible return of the death penalty may be surprised to hear I agree with anything Mark says, but on this we do agree. It is about caring about our children. But the piece of the puzzle that is missing in the views expressed by Mark and others who hold similar views, is that Paul Dally was also once a child. The child he was may be long gone and in his place there may now stand a vicious killer who possibly does need to be kept in prison for the remainder of his natural life, but if other young women are not to suffer Karla's fate, it isn't enough to keep Paul Dally in prison. We must begin to work more effectively with the would-be Paul Dallys currently sitting in our classrooms, living rough on the streets of our towns and cities and working as child prostitutes.

In an interview with Amanda Miller for the *20/20* television programme, the man who headed the investigation into the death of toddler Hinewaoriki Karaitiana-Matiaha (Lillybing), Inspector Rod Drew, was asked what he thought needed to happen to ensure a similar tragedy never happened again. He replied that there must be somebody who is vitally interested in every child every moment of the day. That is exactly what is needed. If as a society we can accept the need to maintain a vital interest in every child born in this country every moment of every day and work together to achieve that aim, the need for more prisons will abate, the number of people whose lives are forever changed by the commission of a violent offence will lessen and the magic that sits inside every child born in New Zealand will have the opportunity to flourish.

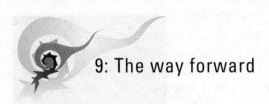

9: The way forward

So where do we begin; how do we even start to make a difference in a society where children who have not yet celebrated their fifteenth birthday are being arrested for murder, where 11-year-old children are prostituting themselves on the streets of our major cities and where 5-, 6- and 7-year-old children are being identified by teachers as likely candidates for prison in the not-too-distant future? The New Zealand population is estimated to rise by 8 per cent by the year 2010 while the country's prison population is expected to rise by 40 per cent within that time. In the face of such predictions, there is the very practical question of just what proportion of our taxes we want to spend on building prisons rather than on schools and kindergartens, but there are two more fundamental questions. What can we do as individuals, as members of our various communities and as members of New Zealand society as a whole, to make the world a safer place for our children and grandchildren? And what can we do to unleash the magic that exists within every child born in this country, rather than allowing so many of them to die prematurely or come to know the inside of a prison cell before their twentieth birthday?

I found it interesting that on *Morning Report* on the Radio NZ National Programme on 30 January 2002, the Leader of the Opposition, Bill English, made the statement that: 'Life for life might not lower the number of murders, but it will make people feel safer in their homes.' He had announced the previous day that if elected to government, the National Party will introduce 'life means life' sentences for the worst murderers. While I am sure the idea of being safer in our homes is appealing to us all, I know with absolute certainty that were either of my children to be murdered, the fact the killer might then be in prison for the rest of his or her life would do little to relieve my pain and return my world to the way it was before the tragedy. I believe we all accept the reality that when someone is murdered, the victim's family and friends serve the true life sentence. Surely the issue is not about feeling safer in our homes once a murder has been committed, but rather is about preventing the murder in the first place.

As I began the process of writing this book, I was very clear I would not be attempting to provide definitive answers to the issues the book would raise. I don't believe I have the answers nor do I believe any one person has them. I have some ideas, but that is all they are at this stage, ideas.

In my view, the answers lie in all of us who live in New Zealand, but more particularly middle New Zealand, combining resources and asking the questions that need to be asked. It requires us to have the courage to pause a while and take note of the issues as they really are, not as we might wish them to be in order that we might remain within our comfort zones. We also need to accept that this isn't a problem for which a quick-fix solution can be found. If we really want New Zealand society to be a safer place for our children and grandchildren, if we do want our taxes to be spent on something other than prisons, we have some work to do.

It isn't going to be an easy task, in fact I believe for a time it will continue to seem an insurmountable problem, but I firmly believe it is 'do-able'. If I didn't, I wouldn't have bothered to write this book nor would I stand as often as I do to tell the stories of the journeys to prison undertaken by so many of our children. I believe that if, as a society, we accept the challenge now in front of us to adopt a holistic and long-term approach to the issues behind the increasing levels of violence in our communities and our spiralling imprisonment rate, we can make a difference. As Rachel Hunter told us all in the shampoo advertisement some years ago: 'It won't happen overnight, but it will happen.'

The public speaking I am now involved in began when I stood to speak to the audiences who attended the performances of the production Kia Maumahara undertaken at Christchurch Women's Prison in 1997. My decision to stand up at the end of each performance and have the final word was born not out of my need to have the final word per se (well, not totally . . .) but rather out of my desire to ensure the audience left the prison with as clear a sense as possible of the part they would play in determining whether the plans made by the women as they prepared to return to their communities at the completion of their sentence would come to fruition.

During my first two years as manager of Christchurch Women's Prison, I had become increasingly aware of, and angered by, the degree to which the general public seemed to consider they had the right to tell me, and all other prison managers, how prisons should be run. I felt as if almost every decision I made, particularly those relating to the parole of inmates into the community as part of their reintegration plans, had to survive the scrutiny of an uninformed 'Joe Public', and it seemed as if the litmus test for granting inmate paroles had become whether I could adequately defend my decision to grant a parole on the *Holmes* show.

We seemed to have entered the arena of management of prisons by public opinion and I was not impressed. As I had been heard to say on more than one occasion, it seemed as if everyone had an opinion and that those determined to express their opinion publicly were equally determined to ensure no facts got in the way. I think I was eventually shown on national television saying that the public 'had no bloody idea what went on in prisons'. (Not exactly the language my mother had sent me to a Catholic girls' school to learn!)

It was my anger about the public's attitude to inmates and prisons that initially got me to my feet in front of the Canterbury public. I wanted people to know how little they really knew about the reality of prison and the inmates. I wanted them to appreciate the hugely negative impact their own attitudes and opinions were having on the lives of the women under my care, who had never really had a chance in life and were doing their very best to ensure they acquired whatever skills they could that might increase their chances of making a good life for themselves and their children after their release. But while it was anger and a need to defend the women against public opinion that initially got me to my feet, as time went on and I continued to challenge audiences about their views and to articulate the reality of the lives of prison inmates as I saw it, my anger began to abate and I discovered a wonderful thing.

I discovered the conscience of New Zealand. I discovered that as a society we do still have one — a living, beating, easily detectable conscience. Despite the degree to which redneck attitudes seem to gain traction in the media, the majority of people do still care; and as a society we do still want to make a difference to the lives of those less fortunate than ourselves. What I had been interpreting as judgement and condemnation was in fact a lack of understanding and an absence of accurate information. That is why I have taken the time to write this book and why I continue to accept invitations to speak — it is not too late. As a society we have not yet crossed the divide into the world of vengeance and a lack of concern for our fellow human beings. But make no mistake, we are standing on the brink of that divide and we need to make a decision very soon about what we want to happen. In the absence of deliberate action, entry into a world of blame and hatred and revenge, a world that will in time taint us all, is inevitable.

So having discovered we do still care, and there is still time to make a difference, the question becomes what is it we need to do? What will make the difference in the lives of at-risk children who, if no one intervenes effectively in their lives, will go on to terrorise or kill, their victim possibly your son or daughter or my yet-to-be-born grandson or granddaughter? What do we do and where do we begin?

I am sure that in response to that question, some of you will have immediately thought of the shortcomings of the various government agencies; what you consider CYF should be doing and isn't, the deficiencies you see in our education system, the need you see for better coordination between the myriad of agencies working in the field of at-risk children and families.

And in my view you would be right. There are some things that need to change at government agency level. A lot of things are happening, a lot of people who care are doing their best to impact in a positive way on the lives of at-risk children, but it seems to me the 'glue' that would make it all work a little better is missing. Silo funding has produced silo mindsets and as a result, government agencies and the people within them often work in isolation rather than being encouraged or required to work in a holistic way with children, families and other agencies. The perceived lack of resources has meant the development of a 'blame' mentality that assumes those who need help will take more than their share if they have the opportunity to do so, that people in need are automatically out to rip off the system. This often means people on both sides are suspicious of each other and the trust necessary if real change is to happen never develops. It also means a suspicion between agencies and a tendency to hold off on the spending of money within one agency because there is reason to believe another agency might pick up the tab.

In terms of the education system, many teachers feel under siege, overworked and under-appreciated as they continue to grapple with the changing demands of their role. They struggle with the degree to which they have become quasi-social workers and with the fact that for some children, being in their classroom is more about being safe from abuse for a few hours each day than it is about learning. The classroom environment has changed significantly within a very short space of time and the level of sophistication demonstrated by students at an increasingly early age has left some teachers at a loss.

And then there are the politicians. I am sure the shortcomings of the various political parties and the political processes we are subject to have also entered your mind as you have considered the problem and possible solutions. Some of your thoughts will probably be centered on the idea that if only 'they' would get their act together, if only 'they' did what they had been mandated by the voters to do, there would be no problem and all would be well with the world. I have heard it said on a number of occasions that we get the politicians we deserve. I am sure that's true and at times I have found that a very frightening thought as I have watched the behaviour of some of those who have been elected to parliament in the debating chamber.

I have at times been intrigued and at other times concerned as I have watched political debate on television and listened to MPs describing the level of personal abuse they have suffered from their fellow MPs. It seems a major contradiction that while we spend a significant amount of money on anti-bullying strategies in schools and kindergarten and primary school teachers work extremely hard to make respect for others a core message for the children they work with, some politicians speaking in the House indulge in behaviour that wouldn't be tolerated in a kindergarten or school. I am fully aware of the need for political point scoring and I am not naïve enough to suggest a world in which politicians spend their time outlining the virtues of their political opponents, but I don't believe political agendas need to incorporate personal insults or that we need to accept behaviour from those we have elected that we wouldn't accept in a school playground. Mature and robust debate of the issues is surely what politics should and must be about.

I have seen the struggle students in our secondary schools have as they begin to build good decision-making skills when teachers don't model appropriate behaviour and the students are told to 'do what we say, not what we do'. I think perhaps it's time politicians began to own the true impact of their sometimes childish behaviour that is being beamed out from the House into the living rooms of New Zealand.

I am also concerned about the degree to which political point-scoring skews the debate on real issues we as a society need to get our head around. In the *Dominion* newspaper of 16 March 2002, under the headline 'Parole of Slavich killer an insult says Dunne', an article carries the story that United Leader, Peter Dunne, believes the parole of a man who killed Paeroa farmer Steven Slavich in 1991 was a huge insult to the man's family.

I am not deliberately picking on Peter Dunne in this; it just so happens that he has given me an example to use to demonstrate my point. I accept the idea that the parole of Shane Rogers, a man who at the age of 16 years brutally murdered Steven Slavich after he stopped to give Rogers and a friend a lift, could be considered by some to be an insult to the family. However, I would be a lot more convinced of Peter Dunne's sincerity if I wasn't very aware of the fact that this comment was made at the dawn of an election year and voters needed to be wooed. It is often incredibly easy to see the political spin on the story and incredibly difficult to see what the real issue might be. It seems to me that the advent of yet another election year inevitably means an automatic increase in the political spin and an almost-total submerging of the real issues we should be considering.

The same can be said for the article that featured on the front page of the *Dominion* on 5 February 2002 under the headline 'Sent to jail but still free to go out'. In this article, ACT NZ's justice spokesperson, Stephen Franks, played up the idea of inmates being paroled to go shopping, to the movies or to sports events, an idea that will be an automatic affront to most New Zealanders. He was quoted as saying: 'It underlines that the system doesn't actually believe in punishment.' Maybe there are issues about inmates on parole from prison being able to go to the movies, but I believe focusing a discussion on the merits of reintegrative processes on that particular aspect of the parole system is less about the possible weaknesses of the system and more about how to build an election platform capitalising on people's fear and sense of justice.

Parole serves a purpose, a very important purpose, in that it allows the process of reintegration of an inmate, who will be released from prison eventually, to be undertaken in a slow and considered manner. The alternative to a system that allows inmates to be paroled as the date of their release draws near is to simply open the prison gates and let the inmate go on the day their sentence ends. Such a course of action invariably means there are no supports in place and the inmate runs an extremely high risk of committing another crime and returning to prison — possibly having burgled your house on the way. There are numerous arguments for and against parole and the type and frequency of paroles that should be allowed, but none of this was discussed in either of the two articles mentioned above. The politicians appeared to be focused only on getting the headline.

Be that as it may, this is not about whether politicians can learn to behave in more appropriate ways or learn to treat us as thinking adults as we take part in an election. Nor is it about what government agencies need to do differently to make the world a safer place, or even what other people could or should do to make the world a better place while we continue to live as we always have. This is about us, you and I, and what we need to do differently in our day-to-day lives if things are ever to change for the better.

I will share with you at this point that for me on a personal level, the answer lies within women's prisons. I believe we have the ability as a country to become world leaders in the management of women in prison and that in so doing, we have the capacity to impact real societal change.

I have met some tough women in my time in women's prisons, women whose lives are totally chaotic, who are in the grip of a major addiction and who appear completely lost and beyond redemption. But what I have never seen in a women's prison is a woman whose eyes did not light up whenever her children were mentioned. Every woman I have ever met in prison who has children wants a better life for them than she had; every woman I have ever met in prison who has children will do almost anything, accept almost any help offered to ensure her children have a better life. And every woman I have ever met in prison who has children will face the demons she will not face on her own account, if in doing so, she believes she is increasing the chances of her children or grandchildren having a better life than the one she has had.

I spoke earlier of the woman resident at Christchurch Women's Prison who was serving a term of imprisonment with her adult daughter while members of both her immediate and extended family were in prison over the road at Christchurch Men's Prison.

When she arrived in prison during my term as manager, her daughter was already there. In the discussions we had with her after her arrival, she accepted with reluctance the fact that her daughter's drug addiction had led her to prison, but she was also very conscious of her grandson, her daughter's baby boy, and she retained a strong hope that prison was something he would never experience.

This woman was well used to a life of crime and well versed in the reality of prison. In the initial discussions held with her about what she would do to address her offending issues while in prison, she was resistant to the idea of doing anything at all and seemed comfortable with the idea she would simply do her time and return to the life she had been leading prior to imprisonment when she was released. She had tried to live a life free of offending when released from prison the last time, but had found the community unforgiving and her options limited, so had made a conscious choice to continue her drug-dealing and risk imprisonment again. It was only when we mentioned her grandson and asked her if she wanted him to experience prison that she came alive. She was adamant she didn't want him to ever experience being locked in a prison cell and she became quite agitated at the possibility prison might be his destiny.

As we continued to talk to her about the patterns of offending that existed within her family, she became increasingly conscious that prison might indeed be a place her grandson would come to know and increasingly adamant that it would not be. As a result of this conversation, she decided to take part in the production undertaken at the prison in 1999, 'Watea — Pathways to Freedom', and it was as a result of being involved in the production that she came to understand the impact of her crime on her many victims and to know the forces operating in her life from an early age that had determined the path she had taken in life. She often talked both during and after the production of the pain she was experiencing as a result of unravelling the memories of abuse and violence that lay behind her offending and admitted that at times, she was tempted to throw in the towel and return to her old ways. In those moments of temptation, she said, she brought the face of her grandson to the forefront of her mind and in so doing, confirmed her resolve to continue the journey she had begun.

For my part, watching this woman struggle with herself, her personal history and the true impact of her offending on her victims, I realised that when it came down to it, it would make little or no difference what social agencies became involved in the life of her grandson or who tried to intervene to turn him away from the path his mother and grandmother and many other members of his extended family had followed. It seemed there was only one person who could alter this boy's destiny and show him a different path and that was the woman I was looking at, his grandmother. I truly believed then, and still believe now, that she is the only one who has a chance of beating the odds stacked against this little boy and it was a magic moment when she took ownership of that fact and resolved to do just that.

For me, it isn't about 'us' fixing 'them'. It is about empowering those who come from disadvantaged and criminal backgrounds to realise the potential they have to make a difference within their own families. It is about showing them that it can be different and they are the key to that difference. It is about investing them with a sense of themselves and their right to live a life free of hassle and harassment. That is why I consider women's prisons to be the place I would start to impact real societal change. Within almost every one of the so-called criminal families, there is a matriarch and it is she who has the potential to ensure the generations of children yet to be born within the family are offered a destiny different to those who have gone before. The women who come to prison are those matriarchs and in many cases, are raising the criminals of the next generation. If we can accept that fact and find the courage and conviction to work alongside them in that reality rather then condemning them for it, I believe we will begin to make a difference.

So there are things the politicians need to do, there are things the government agencies need to do and there are things I would do were the opportunity to present itself. But what about you and I as individuals? What is it we might need to do differently at a personal level in our daily lives if we are serious about playing a part in societal change?

My work within prisons and among at-risk families has left me with the view that the main thing that needs to happen is an attitudinal shift. That doesn't necessarily mean you have to give up your view that prisons should be tough places or start advocating that offenders should be hugged rather than sent to prison. What it does mean is that in determining your view on criminal justice policies, you need to check whose face comes into your mind's eye when the word 'inmate' is used and when you find yourself advocating for harsher penalties or the death penalty. If the face that comes into your mind is the tattooed face of a gang member or the face of a man who brutally killed a young woman after raping her, the challenge I would issue is to remove that face and replace it with the face of an 11-year-old girl who lives on the streets of Auckland and sleeps in the pipes under those same streets; an 11-year-old girl who survives by agreeing to have sex with men who actively seek out her out; an 11-year-old girl who has no expression on her face and who, when you look in her eyes, shows a knowing well beyond her years and a sorrow too deep to contemplate. If your belief in longer and tougher sentences and your consideration of the return of the death penalty can sustain itself in the face of the image of that young girl, then I will happily concede you are entitled to your view.

Until that time, I will continue to believe your view is ill-considered and not linked to the reality I constantly connected with as I spent time in the prisons in this country.

It is not about excusing the behaviour of offenders or minimising the damage their offending does to the lives of their victims. It is about having the courage to look at all the issues and place the crime in the context of those issues before making up our minds as to the most appropriate response. It is about recognising that if we are the victims of a crime, we are unlikely to ever feel totally satisfied with the penalties imposed and accepting that the wider justice system cannot be based solely on the need for revenge.

It is about admitting the degree to which skin colour and money play a part in determining who gets to go to prison in this country and about recognising that we do not all have the same opportunities, we do not all start life from the same place. It is about stopping long enough to recognise the journey offenders were on when they committed the offence. And in the midst of our fear that they will offend again, will move into our street, will want their children to play with our children, having the courage to consider the journey they may have been on since committing that offence, and allowing them adequate room to rebuild their lives. It is about recognising the courage some of those in prison have shown in being willing to face their demons and demonstrating an equal amount of courage in confronting our own fear and prejudice.

In an article in the *Dominion* on 20 December 2001, it was reported that according to a murder victims' group: 'The Parole Board's decision to keep convicted rapist and murderer Paul Bailey in prison would keep every young girl in New Zealand safe for another year.' With all due respect to the family and friends of Kylie Smith, the young woman Paul Bailey viciously murdered, it seems to me there is no real basis for making such a statement. The viciousness of the crime cannot be denied, but the fact remains that there is no way the level of risk he presents to any young woman now can be determined by a group of people who have little or no knowledge of what he has done in the intervening 10 years. I am not for a moment suggesting Paul Bailey should have been granted parole, I have no knowledge on which to base an opinion either way. My point is that the statement made by the murder victims' group is alarmist and seems to be based more on anger and an understandable need for revenge than on a desire to keep every young girl in New Zealand safe.

No one except the Parole Board, prison authorities and Paul Bailey himself know the journey he has been on since he went into prison. The murder victims' group has the right to believe he should be kept in prison forever, but in my view they do not have the right to assume he has done nothing to address the issues that lay behind his offending since he has been in prison and make public statements based on that assumption. It seems to me the time is right to begin an examination of our motives and to find the courage to admit what is really driving us when we seek the imposition of tougher penalties or seek to make ourselves feel good by telling ourselves how much better we are than those who are or have been in prison.

I watched with interest the campaign that was carried out on Auckland's North Shore early in 2001 to try to force Mark Stephens, the man dubbed the Parnell Panther, to move from Browns Bay, a campaign that included a leaflet drop informing his neighbours about his presence. He had been released from prison in 1992 and other than a discharged conviction for disorderly behaviour in 1995, hadn't been charged with a serious crime since his release. It was an easy campaign to run, one that capitalised on people's existing fears and generated more without too much effort.

I don't believe the campaign was based on the degree of threat Mark presented to his female neighbours, given his previous offences. I believe it had to do with his perceived temerity in believing he was entitled to live in a white middle-class North Shore neighbourhood. Had he remained on the other side of the bridge, in Otara, Mangere or Manurewa, no one would have noticed or cared. It was when he dared to believe he had paid his dues to society and could live unfettered by his past that something had to be done to remind him we would never forgive him, would never let him be one of us, would always consider ourselves to be better than him irrespective of anything he might do to make amends and rebuild his life.

As I think about our reaction to ex-inmates living in our street, I recall the story of one woman I met in prison. She had come from a city suburb in which many at-risk families lived. While in prison, she did every self-development course that was offered, she took out a non-molestation order against her violent husband and she resolved that life would be different for her and her children once she was released. As she contemplated release, she realised a return to the same suburb would mean return to prison as her chances of staying free of drugs and criminal activity in that area were negligible. So she moved into a more upmarket suburb to begin her new life.

After three months in the 'nicer' area, she returned to her former suburb to live, motivated by a sense of loneliness and isolation. Six months later she was again standing in the receiving office in Christchurch Women's Prison.

While it may be enough of a challenge to our sense of how the world should work when ex-inmates want to live in our street, the much bigger challenge we need to face seems to come when there are plans made to build a prison or a youth justice facility in our area. I have found the level of hysteria whipped up when there is the slightest hint of a prison being built in the area quite amazing and very concerning. The 'Not In My Back Yard' syndrome (NIMBY) is certainly alive and well in this country and I am fascinated by the views of those who seem to think prison inmates drop in from another planet to serve their sentence and should return there when they have done so. The unfortunate reality that we all have to grapple with is that these people, those who are serving terms of imprisonment, come from our communities and will return to them when they are released.

If it were not so sad, it might be funny that there are so many signs along the road between Auckland and Hamilton addressing the possibility of a prison being built near Meremere. One of the signs I saw the last time I drove that stretch of road actually said 'No Auckland criminals in the Waikato'. I couldn't believe my eyes. New Zealand is a village and here we are trying to assign criminals to specific geographical areas. I am sorry if I offend some people by saying so, but the only response I can make to the suggestion that a prison should not be built in the Waikato because it might end up housing criminals from Auckland is to suggest you get over yourselves. We have a problem and it belongs to us all, not least the white middle- and upper-class New Zealanders who, by virtue of the family they were born into rather than anything they themselves have done, have started life in a better place than many of the people who will find their way into the prison that might be built at Meremere. To suggest that one geographical area look after it's 'own' criminals is to completely ignore the part we all play in condemning 10-, 11- and 12-year-old children to a life on the streets. I wonder how many children who were born in the Waikato have left the home in which they were neglected and abused to take up a life on the streets of Auckland?

There is no doubt in my mind that it will be when an

attitudinal shift occurs at an individual level that, as a society, we will begin to make the real difference to the futures of the children yet to be born in this country. But I am also aware that this attitudinal shift will the hardest thing to achieve.

As a country we are used to being innovative in a practical sense — the 'number eight' fencing wire approach has worked well in the past and no doubt will continue to do so when there are practical things to be done. I am not so convinced we are robust enough to face our own prejudices and accept that for many, this country isn't the paradise we would like to think it is.

As I watch the ongoing debate about the state of our criminal justice system, I find myself thinking that as a culture we are a lot like a 15-year-old adolescent. We want to be treated like adults, are constantly telling anyone who will listen that we are adults, but when trouble hits we revert to being children. We all take pride in winning the America's Cup; we're all happy to claim ownership of *The Lord of the Rings*. But when the other side of life pops up, the heavier side, the reality that we all play a part in the violent deaths of some of our children and in the creation of some of the monsters in our prisons, we want to retreat to our bedroom like an adolescent who's just put a dent in the car they insisted they were old enough to drive.

For my part, I will know we have grown up as a society, that we are now adults willing to accept the good and the bad in life and willing to maximise the opportunities in front of us, when the fights that occur over any new prison, sex offenders unit or youth justice facility occur because too many communities want the facility built in their area, and when the media displays clear evidence that as a society we fully understand the part we play in the journeys taken to prison by our youth.

While the bulk of what needs to be done sits at an individual level, I believe there is also work we can be doing as a society at a national level. At the moment we are virtually held to ransom by a three-year election cycle. The politicians tell us via their election promises what they think they can deliver within the looming three-year term; we vote for them according to the appeal of their promises and they deliver what they can (not usually all they promised). As the next election approaches, the cycle begins again. A simplistic approach to a complicated issue perhaps, but nonetheless a reflection of the process as I see it and as it impacts on me in my day-to-day life. My concern as I have continued my attempts to come to terms with the way in which politics works and have tried to match political reality to the reality I have been faced with in prisons is that we, the community, seem to be at the mercy of the politicians, rather than the other way around.

We vote for them, they are there to deliver what it is *we* think the country needs to flourish and yet it seems to me we often fail to hold them fully to account. Policies come and go against the backdrop of an election every three years, everything is managed within a very short timeframe and with an almost tunnel-like vision and we buy into it, or perhaps more accurately, we apathetically accept that is how it has to be.

So why do we accept it and does it really have to be that way? Am I being incredibly naïve in my belief that there has to be a way in which we, the voters, can exercise a greater degree of ownership of and a greater degree of responsibility for this country's policies? We are after all the voters, the ones who elect the politicians. As I have continued to ponder this issue, I've wondered what would keep us involved beyond the few months that surround an election, as we try to decide who to vote for, and what would be required if the country were to adopt a vision for the country that lasted beyond the three-year election cycle.

What if we, the voters, designed and took ownership of a 20-year strategy, a strategy that took into account the fact that not all problems can be solved overnight? A strategy that recognised that while early intervention is the obvious mechanism with which to achieve maximum impact in the lives of disadvantaged children, money still needs to be spent, at least in the interim, on prisons and at various points in between? What if the strategy was owned by the community rather than by the politicians? Against the backdrop of such a strategy, informed decisions could be made about the sequence in which the various societal problems were to be addressed and as an election approached, evaluations of the various political candidates and parties could be made against where they felt energy, in terms of the strategy, should be directed for the next three years. The essence of this idea is that we would lead the politicians rather than the politicians leading us.

I am not sure how or when it happened, but from where I'm sitting, it seems we have become victims waiting to be saved by the politicians, angry when they don't save us or when they don't do it quickly enough or in the way we wanted. Perhaps it's time we stood up, reclaimed what it is to be a New Zealander and began the task, the very difficult task, of preparing a better society for the generations of New Zealanders that will follow us. I am not sure at this stage how the development of the 20-year strategy might begin, but I do have a strong sense it is possible and I am sure Kiwi ingenuity would find a way if it was something we believed in and were prepared to commit to.

I have told various stories throughout this book and I am going to tell one more to finish this chapter in the hope that this story will leave you with the sense that however difficult the wider issues appear, the part you can play with maximum impact is very easy to learn. The story was given to me by someone who had listened to me speak about community attitudes towards ex-inmates.

A woman was sitting in a 5 Series BMW outside a service station waiting for her husband when a couple walked towards the car. They were dressed in black and had tattoos and quite an aggressive manner. As they moved towards the BMW, the woman in the car heard one of them say in a loud and aggressive tone: 'Where d'ya get that car?' For a brief second the woman paused and noted her sense of discomfort at having drawn the couple's attention, then looked directly at the couple, smiled and said: 'Out of a Weet-Bix packet.' The woman who had asked the question laughed and replied: 'And I suppose you got your licence out of a Kornies packet?' Everyone laughed together for a minute and then the moment was gone.

The woman in the BMW had stepped over her fear and connected for a moment with people who, just as she was, were making their way through life as best they could and with the skills they had at hand. We don't have to be everybody's friend, but we can learn where our prejudices sit, recognise the advantages we have had and accept our part in making the difference to the lives of those who have not been so lucky.

It starts with a smile.

10: One year on . . .

Just on a year ago, I began putting the stories and ideas I had been carrying around in my head for quite some time down on paper. The idea that I was capable of writing a book was quite novel and more than a little daunting.

A year later, I am again beginning a writing process; this time I am setting out to write an additional chapter to be included in a new edition.

People have been extremely generous in their response to *The Journey to Prison* and I have been humbled by the reactions of those I have met since its launch. To be told you have written 'a life-changing' book, to have people acknowledge that they started the book with one opinion on the issues of law and order and social justice and finished it with another is an extraordinary gift. I am indebted to all those who have shared their reaction to the book with me. Thank you.

I have been asked a number of times whether there is another book 'in there' and my answer has been and will remain a resounding no. I consider myself a writer and a teller of stories rather than an author and I have now told the stories. Perhaps in another 20 years there will be more stories to tell and another book will emerge, but in the meantime it is time to return to the work itself and to consider in what way I might make a worthwhile and real contribution to the world into which my yet-to-be conceived grandchildren will be born.

If there isn't another book in there, why am I sitting down to write again? Primarily because there is another chapter that needs to be written, a chapter which examines some of the issues raised in the book in the light of subsequent events. These include the conviction of 13-year-old Bailey Junior Kurariki for the part he played in the death of Michael Choy and the issues raised by the conviction of several other youngsters for violent crimes; the election results; the release of high profile inmates Gay Oakes and Tania Witika from Christchurch Women's Prison and ongoing media debate over the building of new prisons.

For my part, this allows me the opportunity to re-examine my thinking on social justice issues in light of what 2002 delivered and to consider again just what we need to do to save the young children within our communities who are currently at risk of coming to prison. Of course, the ultimate aim is to save not only the children, but also their potential victims.

On the evening of Saturday 24 August 2002, the face of 13-year-old Bailey Junior (BJ) Kurariki was revealed on television for the first time. He, along with six other teenagers aged between 15 and 17 years, had been on trial in the High Court in Auckland for the murder of Michael Choy. Earlier that day he had been found guilty of manslaughter for the part he played in Michael's death. One of the accused was found not guilty, while a 17-year-old girl and a 16-year-old boy were found guilty of murder and the remaining accused, including BJ, were found guilty of manslaughter. At the time he committed the offence, BJ was 12 years of age.

As I saw him for the first time, I was struck, as I am sure all those watching the evening news were, by his cherubic face. There is really no other word that captures the essence of the face that stared at the world through a camera lens, seemingly unaware of or unaffected by the impact he was having on the many people struggling to come to grips with the fact that someone so young could be involved in so brutal a crime. The following morning as I picked up a copy of the *Sunday Star-Times*, reality slammed home again with the same face taking up a significant proportion of the front page.

162

When I stood in front of a group of people in April 2001 and made the statement about a blond, angelic-faced 5-year-old boy sitting in a classroom in New Zealand who was on his way to prison and was likely to kill someone along the way, I hadn't said it in an attempt to hit the headlines, but because I believed then, and still do, that not one but several 5-, 6- and 7-year-old children sitting in classrooms around the country at that time were leading lives that were predestining them for prison.

I made the statement out of a sense of anger and concern that the magic that lies within all children at birth was being so needlessly lost from so many while we continued to argue the merits of longer prison sentences. Within 18 months of making that statement in an attempt to rouse us all, myself included, out of our complacency about the cause of our rising prison population, along with most of middle New Zealand I was rendered speechless by the face of a 13-year-old boy convicted of manslaughter.

The caption that ran with the photo in the *Sunday Star-Times* on Sunday 25 August 2002 said it all: 'At 9 he was shoplifting, by 10 he was banned from school, at 12 he helped kill a pizza delivery man.' In the story that accompanied the headline, we learned that BJ had been known to the police from the age of 9 and had been suspended from primary school six months into standard four, by which stage he was 10 years old. Child, Youth and Family Service staff had been working with BJ and his family, primarily his father and sister, for 'a little over two years' and he was apparently on the run from a social welfare home at the time of the murder.

A number of things occurred to me in the aftermath of learning the identity of the 12-year-old boy whose 'small, slight and young' appearance had caused gasps of shock as he stood in the dock in Papakura Youth Court, as described in Chapter 8. My primary response was to wonder how we as a society could get it so wrong that a boy who was causing concern by the age of 9 was able to continue on his way until the age of 12 with such devastating consequences.

The obvious answer, or perhaps more correctly the easiest answer, is that one person or one government agency was to blame and in the days following the release of BJ's identity, there was considerable discussion in the media, that seemed to me to focus more on the allocation of blame rather than the need to find out how things might have been done differently. The primary focus was on his family and on Child, Youth and Family Services (CYF). Under the headline 'Welfare failed boy killer: police officer', an article in the *New Zealand Herald* on 26 August 2002 quoted a policeman 'who tried to save New Zealand's youngest killer from a cycle of chronic offending' as saying that CYF had failed the boy because social workers had not followed through on plans for BJ's care and rehabilitation.

Information contained in articles in the *Sunday Star-Times* on 25 August and the *New Zealand Herald* on 26 August exposed us to enough of the family background to give us reason to suppose the family were to blame, an impression strengthened by the extremely unflattering photo of BJ's mother, Lorraine West, that appeared inside the *Sunday Star-Times*. It seemed to me to be a photo Lorraine wasn't happy to have taken and was, for me, evidence of the cruelty the media is capable of when it suits.

As I paused to wonder at the life of the woman into whose worn face I was looking as I gazed at the photo, I imagined people reading the paper over a relaxed Sunday morning coffee who would see the photo and shrug off any responsibility for the fact this country now had a 13-year-old killer among its crime statistics. I could see them thinking the involvement of BJ in Michael Choy's murder was obviously down to bad parenting, and if there was residual blame needing to be assigned elsewhere, it could be directed towards CYF.

It is highly likely that if what has been reported in the media to date is correct, some of the blame for BJ's offending may very well be slated home to his parents and some to CYF. While this may be the case, however, my thoughts continue to centre on the degree to which attempts to allocate blame deflect us from the real task at hand if we are to prevent other youngsters going the same way, and avoid the pain of senseless and violent deaths like that of Michael Choy.

I tell myself it can't be that hard, there has to have been an answer, something we missed or could have done better. And in using the pronoun 'we', I mean you and I. Much as we might not want to be, we are all in this and we pay the price as a society when something like this happens.

He may have been an 'extremely difficult child' (CYF, *New Zealand Herald* 26 August 2002) and 'easily the most experienced criminal of those on trial for the Choy murder' (Police, *New Zealand Herald* 26 August 2002), but BJ was, after all is said and done, just a boy and it is difficult to believe we don't have what it takes to wrap around children such as him and save them from themselves. This is Godzone territory after all; we do so many things so well. Why can't we prevent children from being involved in senseless murders, as so many have been in recent times?

There is no simple answer and I haven't written this additional chapter in order to provide you with one. I am still focused on the complexity of the question and am disappointed to see the degree to which the efforts expended in the aftermath of such cases continue to centre on allocating blame rather than examining the real questions the situation raises. And once the blame has been assigned to our apparent satisfaction, albeit quickly and relatively superficially, moves are then made to eliminate further criticism of politicians and government policy by the announcement of a solution we are expected to believe will adequately address the issue.

In the aftermath of BJ's conviction, Justice Minister Phil Goff was quoted in the *Dominion Post* of 26 August 2002 saying that in several Government initiatives on teenage offending, he had delivered an edict that departments must communicate more openly with each other. 'One initiative is Youth Offending Teams in every police district, which will integrate the work of police, Child

Youth and Family and the Health and Education departments.' In the article, the Minister adds, 'The left hand will know what the right hand is doing in regard to those kids.'

There are several questions posed by Mr Goff's announcement, not least how it is that the left hand doesn't already know what the right hand is doing in regard to these kids? Could it be that the means by which government agencies are funded encourage separatist thinking and discourage the establishment of interagency relationships? Could it be that agencies and schools have been forced to become experts in patch protection in order to ensure the resources they have been allocated go as far as necessary in order to achieve the outputs for which they are being held responsible?

My recent experience working among the families of at-risk children has led me to believe that interagency cooperation is sorely lacking and it will take more than an edict from a Government Minister to correct the problem. Let me be clear that this is not a criticism of individual caseworkers. Interagency cooperation is not lacking because those working with at-risk families are deliberately refusing to talk to one another, but because workloads are high, time is of the essence and money is scarce — or is perceived to be scarce. 'Silo' funding has encouraged 'silo' thinking and as a result an expression that now appears to have real currency when help is being sought from an agency by a school or another agency is 'it doesn't meet our threshold'.

In an article in the *Weekend Herald* on 27 July 2002, Dr Ian Lambie, a senior lecturer in clinical psychology at the University of Auckland, agreed with my contention that some people are more likely to offend because the cards are stacked against them and talked about effective community-based programmes already in place. He went on to say that what is needed is more money: 'It's not rocket science. It's a matter of resourcing.'

I agree with Dr Lambie that there are many effective community-based programmes out there, but I do not agree that it is a case of just needing more money. Rather, I think it is a case of needing to review both how the money is spent and the thinking that currently drives the way the money is spent. There are bucket loads of money out there, but due to the silo mentality that has been cultivated within government agencies, the resulting duplication of administrative systems, the output-driven nature of the work being done by agency workers and the degree to which those working with at-risk families are being held to ransom by the Privacy Act, a considerable amount is either being wasted or could be spent more effectively. Put simply, people working within the agencies must be given permission and the time to talk to one another about the work they are doing and the need to build effective relationships with clients and colleagues must be validated to a far greater degree than it is currently.

The 'blame' culture is also doing considerable damage and our politicians often appear to be leading the charge, presumably driven by a perceived need to satisfy our ever-present desire for vengeance and revenge and thus ensure their re-election. I am sometimes reminded of the women knitting in front of the guillotine in the French Revolution as I listen to media discussions about who is to be blamed for what when yet another violent crime comes to light.

It was with considerable concern that I heard Social Services Minister Steve Maharey state on the *Late Edition News* on TV One on Thursday 5 December 2002, following the conviction of Bruce Howse for the murder of his two stepdaughters, that 'if someone has made a mistake, we will find that person'. He was referring to a breakdown in communications that had apparently occurred between CYF and the mother of the murdered girls, Charlene Aplin, a breakdown that may have led to Bruce Howse opening a letter addressed to Charlene containing allegations of sexual abuse by him against one of her daughters, a week before they were murdered.

There are, quite rightly, investigations now underway on this matter and if it did happen, steps need to be taken to understand how and why and to ensure it can never happen again. My concern with Mr Maharey's statement on this occasion is that in making it, he took us a considerable distance towards the idea that an individual is to blame rather than a system or a government policy and by so doing, reinforced the blame culture already prevalent in our society. Perhaps an individual social worker did make an error of judgement, but what about the possibility that workload issues and pressure from the social worker's supervisor to get the matter sorted meant that after failing on a number of occasions to meet face-to-face with Charlene Aplin, the social worker felt they had no option but to write the letter?

I know no more about this case than anyone else who has followed the story in the media, but what I do know from personal experience is that CYF social workers are under enormous pressure and their workloads allow little time to build the relationships that are an absolute prerequisite if they are to effectively get alongside the mothers of at-risk children. I do know the degree to which some mothers work to avoid any contact with CYF or any other government agency because of the negative experiences they have had in the past. And I do know that having a Government Minister speak about the matter in a way that suggests a witch-hunt may well be under way cannot do much to engender a sense of being supported in their work among the CYF social workers who struggle every day to do their best for the children they work with.

One senior CYF social worker I met on a plane a few months ago told me she had just resigned. When I asked why, she said she joined the organisation to work with children and was leaving because her job no longer allowed her to do so. She went on to say her primary relationship was now with her computer as she sought to meet the bureaucratic demands of her position.

I don't condone sloppy work by social workers that puts children at risk, but nothing I have seen to date tells me that social workers are deliberately sloppy. What I have seen is a system that doesn't validate the work involved in the establishment and management of effective relationships with at-risk families, a system that is output- rather than outcome-driven and a system that moves quickly to assure itself (and us) when something goes wrong that the mistake is down to the individual involved rather than a result of the way the wider system is operating.

With regard to the establishment and management of effective relationships, I want to return to the initiative Justice Minister Phil Goff spoke of in the *Dominion Post* of 26 August 2002, two days after BJ Kurariki had been found guilty. He told us youth offending teams in every police district would integrate the work of police, CYF and the Ministries of Health and Education.

It's a great idea and one that makes a lot of sense. There is a problem with it though, at least from where I'm sitting. As I understand it, the idea has its genesis in the Youth Crime Taskforce Report presented by then Principal Youth Court Judge David Carruthers to Mr Goff at the end of 2001. While it is a great idea, it is one that needs to be worked through in terms of how to begin or continue the process of relationship building between government departments, what adjustment to work practices of the various agencies might be necessary and what resourcing issues it might raise.

To have the announcement about the establishment of the youth offending teams appear in the media just two days after BJ was found guilty certainly alerted my suspicions about how much real impact these teams might have on youth offending as opposed to perceived impact. Was I looking at yet another attempt to pay lip service to the voters, I asked myself, as I attempted to focus on the enormous potential such an initiative has to do good *if* it is implemented properly, i.e. with the appropriate amount of forethought and planning.

I managed to control my scepticism for a short time, but not for long. In an article in the *Dominion Post* on 31 August 2002 headed 'How politicians contribute to crime', Greg O'Connor, head of the Police Association, talked about the establishment of the youth offending teams and made the comment that in response to the announcement by the Minister, police commanders 'trying to put sufficient police on the road to protect the public let out a collective groan'. He went on to say that while the idea was highly commendable, in reality it meant 30 police officers would have to be 'plucked from frontline policing' to head the teams and no doubt managers in the various other sectors that had been targeted would be 'equally hard-pressed to decide what area will receive reduced service so the minister's political decree can be obeyed'.

Subsequent discussions with some of those who work in the various government departments involved in the youth offending teams revealed that it appeared to have become largely a tick-the-box exercise. The political decree apparently included the fact that meetings of the relevant agency personnel were to be held in the various regions by a nominated date, which was less than three months after the initial announcement; no doubt so the Minister could then respond to any questions asked in the House about action being taken by the government on youth offending that the teams were in place . . . political risk managed, problem solved, no need to talk any more about where we as a society might have failed BJ and his co-offenders. It would seem my scepticism has plenty of fertile ground in which to continue to grow!

It is entirely possible that the teams will make a difference and we will eventually see an effective process wrapping around at-risk children in operation. Unfortunately it is equally possible the concept will never work to its full potential because it was introduced with speed and without due thought in order to meet a political agenda. I would like to believe success is possible, but I remain highly sceptical about that because on the basis of what I have seen to date, it seems we continue to seek instant solutions and allow political expediency to drive the process.

Before leaving the issue of BJ behind, I want to make mention of the furore that erupted in the media in November 2002 when it became known that All Blacks Aaron and Nathan Mauger had visited BJ in Christchurch's Kingslea Residential Centre. The generosity of spirit that led the Mauger brothers to make the visit cannot be denied and it is unfortunate if the resulting publicity left them feeling they were being criticised for that generosity. The issues I grappled with in the aftermath of hearing about the visit did not concern the Maugers, they related entirely to CYF's handling of the issue.

I don't deny the value of putting positive role models in front of young offenders whose view of the world and the place they might occupy in it is likely to be extremely narrow, particularly role models who are real in the way the All Blacks are to most boys in New Zealand. Nor do I see anything inherently wrong if BJ was just one of a group of 13 or so youngsters who met the Mauger brothers. What concerns me on the basis of my contact with 15- and 16-year-old offenders while at Christchurch Women's Prison is that if those overseeing the programme BJ is a part of at Kingslea consider there is real value in putting him in front of positive role models this early in his sentence — less than three months into a seven-year term of imprisonment — then, in my opinion, it is possible they may not fully appreciate the complexities that will be involved in the rehabilitation of this boy.

In my experience, it is not enough to stand in front of these kids, (and they are just kids, despite the apparent sophistication of their behaviour), and say this is how you need to be living your life from now on; you too can be a positive and contributing member of society. In each young offender I met in Christchurch Women's Prison or on the rare occasion at Kingslea, it was possible to detect layer upon layer of hurt and anger under which sat deep, festering wounds. Rather than attempting to put more Band-aids across the wounds as the exposure to role models too early might, any help given in the early stages of their sentence needs to focus on peeling back the layers at a pace that allows the child to really feel the pain he or she has buried deep inside and then offering an appropriate level of support when they show they are ready to move through the pain and out the other side. It is as they do this that they come truly to terms with the pain and misery they have inflicted on others.

The All Blacks no doubt have hero status as far as BJ is concerned and every boy needs a hero, but surely there is merit in pausing long enough to allow those who will be working with this child to come to know him, and to allow him to come to terms with where he is, before exposing him to potential role models. I often felt when managing youth offenders that they were way ahead of us in terms of their sophistication and degree of 'street cred'. This, coupled with an extreme naivety in other respects due to their lack of education and the complete absence of two-way discussions with the adults in their lives, meant they were a definite challenge when it came to finding a way to lead them towards a crime-free existence. To date there has been nothing in the reported management of BJ that reassures me CYF have been able to lift their game to the necessary level to manage him effectively. If they had, we would not be hearing so much about him in the media; he would simply have disappeared off the radar screen.

In one of the television news items I watched in the aftermath of the revelation that the Mauger brothers had visited Kingslea, I recall the CYF spokesperson saying something to the effect of 'it is not our concern if BJ's mother showed the photo to the media'. I disagree — it is totally CYF's concern, or at least it should be. Lorraine West has been demonised by the media and it would seem on the basis of information revealed in the media that her relationship with CYF in the months preceding BJ's arrest was not a good one, Lorraine having accused CYF of going behind the family's back to make her son a state ward. The state sought to intervene and now has custody of the child, albeit after an extremely sad series of events. To my mind, as those now responsible for his welfare, CYF had an absolute obligation to advise Lorraine of the likely reaction if she showed the photo of BJ and the Maugers to a reporter.

Management of the media was and is always going to be a part of managing BJ — you only have to whisper his name and media interest is aroused. My challenge to CYF is that they need to be able to demonstrate a better understanding than they have shown to date of the complexity of the lives of the young offenders now coming to notice and to have management plans in place which recognise that complexity and the potential influence of the media on the journey these youngsters will need to take as part of their recovery.

As the furore about the Mauger's visit to Kingslea died down, we were treated to the news that 'famous United States horse whisperer Monty Roberts could be turning his charm on youth prisoner Bailey Kurariki', (*Daily News* 12 November 2002), and on television items on *Holmes* on 27 November 2002 and on TV3 on 1 December 2002, we had it confirmed first that Monty intended to visit Kingslea and then that he had visited.

Among the views that Monty shared with us in the Paul Holmes interview was the fact that 'within these walls there are precious people who need help' and that he intended to 'look them in the eye and tell them my principles — that violence is never the answer'. After his visit to Kingslea on 1 December, he announced on the TV3 news item that he had been in a room with 13 kids and for all he knew 'they could all be murderers'. He didn't care, he 'just knows they are in trouble and they need help and that is what my mission is'. When asked in the *Holmes* interview about his rate of success with the children he had visited to date, he stated that his success rate among children such as those he was intending to visit at Kingslea was 'huge'. We also learned he has recently written a book that expands on his ideas of how the principles involved in the management of difficult horses can be applied to people.

As I watched the various news clips, I began to feel real anger at what I saw as the significant risk of turning the young offenders being spoken about into showpieces. The idea that someone can drop into the lives of these children for an hour or two and affect real change is so ludicrous as to be laughable and I would laugh except that I remember the reality of the lives of the damaged children I met in Christchurch Women's.

These children don't need yet another adult dropping into their lives and sharing their ideas about how to live life, particularly someone from overseas who can have little or no understanding of the reality of their lives and whose message to them is simply that 'violence isn't the answer'. This is an entirely different proposition to the idea of role models such as the Mauger brothers making a visit. Monty is a man the children he is visiting are likely to know little about who dropped into their lives for a hour or two and then talks about the difference he made in some of their lives.

Monty may be a very nice man and he may have very good intentions, but his visit to Kingslea left me with some serious concerns. Having taken the time to log onto to his website, I can confirm that he does indeed talk about his visit to Kingslea. Under the heading 'Monty Roberts' Green Stone', he tells of his visits to the John Oxley Detention Centre in Brisbane and to Kingslea, which he calls the 'Christchurch Youth Detention Centre'. He plays up the size of the institution and makes the statement that 'they have some real toughs there'. He goes on to make some very generalised comments about Maori, a number of which I consider at the very least misleading, and claims about the children he spoke to and the real difference he made in the lives of some of them, claims I find difficult to believe.

Without doubt, these kids will have had any number of five-minute-wonder adults in their lives, adults who have wanted to help, but who have not been willing or able to stick around when the going got tough; I have to wonder where CYF staff's heads are at if they cannot see the harm they are doing by allowing visits such as this to go ahead. When will we stop giving our power away to overseas experts, I ask myself, and when will we come to realise that we have the ability to find our own workable solutions to our own very real problems? When will we realise that there are no instant and easy solutions, that we will only begin to impact real societal change when we commit to being in the lives of these children for the long haul?

When I began writing this book in January 2002, I was very conscious we were entering an election year. There had been some thought that the book might make it onto the shelves in time to contribute to the pre-election debate, but the book was launched in August, just a few weeks after the election. Now a few months on, it is interesting to look back and see just what that election delivered.

I am not about to undertake an in-depth analysis of the election process or results, that has been done (to death, some would say) and I am not appropriately qualified for the task, but I would like to talk for a moment about my overall impressions. For what was probably only the second time in my life, I paid close attention in the pre-election period to what was being said and what was being promised and as the process continued, I began to once again despair at the quality of debate around law and order issues. I found myself agreeing wholeheartedly with a statement by Greg O'Connor, head of the Police Association, in an article that appeared in the *Dominion Post* on 18 June 2002, that it was proving to be a 'fear of crime election'.

The promises made throughout the election campaign seemed to be based entirely on the need for punishment and revenge. All political parties seemed to be focusing on longer prison sentences and the need to ensure offenders spend more of their sentence locked in a small prison cell. Finlay MacDonald, editor of the *Listener,* put it well when in an editorial on 7 September 2002 he spoke of 'an election campaign characterised by fire-and-brimstone sermonising from the get-tough-on-crime preachers'.

One party promised us that if we gave them three years in power, they would 'fix' the problem of law and order (Can we fix it? Yes we can!), while another spoke of the need to ensure the first half of any inmate's prison sentence consisted of hard labour because that approach 'had worked overseas'. Both ideas are in my view a complete nonsense, but they do make us feel better, don't they? Simple solutions that let us off the hook . . . for a minute or two anyway. It became an election of slogans and one-liners designed to have maximum impact in the 30-second sound bite. And we bought it — the election results show us that.

We can complain all we like about the election and the lack of real debate on the issues, but the fact is we bought into it, in some instances in a very big way, and got both the level of election debate we wanted and the results we deserved. Debate stayed focused on the short-term issues and in some very clear instances, the slogans, the one-liners and the 30-sound bites worked.

I have been reasonably critical of Justice Minister Phil Goff and Social Services Minister Steve Maharey earlier in this chapter in terms of the public responses they made to issues raised in the aftermath of the murders of Michael Choy and sisters Saliel Aplin and Olympia Jetson, but there is something of which you and I need to remain fully aware. The Ministers made the responses they did at those times because that is exactly what we, the general public, wanted them to do. We want government ministers to tell us everything is all right and there is nothing we need to be doing, no changes we need to be making to the way we live our lives; we want their reassurance that whatever is happening out there, whatever violence is being perpetrated, however many children are making an early entrance into the criminal justice system, there is nothing we need to be doing — they are doing it, they are taking care of the problem for us.

If the problems that led to a 12-year-old boy being found guilty of manslaughter can be fixed by a Ministerial edict that government departments are to begin talking to one another and if the problems that led to two young girls being murdered in their beds can be fixed by finding the social worker to blame, we are off the hook. We don't have to examine ourselves, our lives or our commitment to those who live within our local community. Making decisive statements that get us off the hook is what gets politicians re-elected — we have the proof.

I have talked before about the passionate belief I have in the potential of women in prison, believing as I do in the particular combination of magic and courage that is contained within a women's prison and seeing women in prison as a starting point as we begin to grapple with the issues raised by a burgeoning imprisonment rate. They are, after all, raising the criminals of the next generation.

While she has never been a prison inmate, as I have watched the story of Lorraine West, BJ Kurariki's mother, unfold in the media, I have been re-affirmed in my belief that the mothers at the centre of at-risk families are the place to start. Women in prison in New Zealand have always been, and to my mind remain, the forgotten ones, the add-ons to the male prison system whose differing needs are not adequately recognised and/or worked with in the course of their prison sentence. Despite whatever superficial steps might appear to have been taken in recent times to identify and address the specific needs of women in prison, I believe there is a long way to go before it will be anything more than lip service.

My focus now is on the establishment of an organisation that will in time become an effective voice for women in prison and for the women at the centre of the at-risk families in our communities, an organisation that empowers women in the raising of their children and that can lend itself to and encourage sensible discussion around law and order issues.

In the spirit of such an organisation, there are some comments I need to make on the recent release of high-profile inmates Tania Witika and Gay Oakes from Christchurch Women's Prison.

Tania Witika was released late in 2002 after serving one of the longest finite terms of imprisonment imposed in this country, a term of 15 years and 9 months imposed after the death of her daughter Delcelia. There was a great deal of media interest in Tania's release and I learned when talking to her some weeks after her release that the media interest was continuing, and proving to be extremely intrusive. We were told via print media on the day following her release that she left the institution in a limousine, the implication being as I saw it that she saw no reason to bow her head and leave prison quietly despite the part she had played in her daughter's horrific death. In my view it was a case of a woman who had been demonised in the press many times since her sentence began being demonised yet again.

Perhaps you are thinking that the interest in Tania's release was appropriate, the reporting of her departure from the institution in a limousine valid. Maybe it was. What wasn't reported, though, was that while she may have left the institution in a limousine, Tania did not then go and get drunk or high to celebrate her release from prison as many newly released inmates do and as you and I might be tempted to do in similar circumstances. What did she do? She told me she went to work. She had been attending a work release programme prior to her release from prison and on the day she was released, she went to work as usual.

How many people would have the self-discipline to do as Tania did, I ask myself, after being in prison for over 10 years? As Tania explained it to me, she wants to be a contributing member of society and wants to be able to use her experiences to help other women in violent domestic situations before they or their children die and she considered the first step in putting the pieces of her life back together involved keeping her job.

The other point I would like to make in relation to the approach taken by the media to Tania's release is that she had a co-offender. Eddie Smith was charged with exactly the same crime as Tania, was judged to be equally culpable and received the same sentence. If I am correct in my recall as to how sentencing works, the fact Eddie got exactly the same sentence as Tania will have meant that unless he had his release delayed due to misconduct while in prison, he would have been released on the same day. Yet nowhere in the media have I seen any reference to where he is at present. Why is that?

The answer — from my perspective — is quite simple. The media's job is to talk to us about that which interests us. Like the politicians, the media are our servants and just as the politicians have learned what it is we like to hear, the media have learned what it is we like to read about in our newspapers and see on our television news programmes. The media know we are not particularly interested in what Eddie Smith might be doing or even if he has, in fact, been released from prison. We are far more interested in a mother who, we have heard time and again, partied while her abused and neglected daughter died. It would seem Eddie's culpability in the death of Delcelia has been forgotten while Tania continues to pay the price for what she did.

This is the 'stuff' of the lives of women who have been in prison in this country. Eddie Smith will probably slip back into his life on the outside with no one really being aware or caring who he is, while Tania lives her day-to-day life in anticipation of the inevitable moment when a television camera will capture her on film as she shops in the supermarket or sits with friends in a café and then broadcast her image to the nation.

That is exactly what happened to Gay Oakes. A high-profile inmate because of the circumstances of her offending, she was released late in 2002 after serving a term of imprisonment for the murder of her husband. Her release engendered a similar level of media interest to that of Tania with TV crews camped at the prison gates on the day of her release.

I smiled to myself that morning as I watched a television news reporter describe with absolute sincerity on *Breakfast* on TV One that Gay had left the institution several hours earlier and was now no doubt well away from Christchurch. At the time I doubted that would have been the case, and I learned later that at the time the statement was being made on national television, Gay was still in the institution preparing herself for release while discussions were continuing with prison management as to how to get her out without the media catching a glimpse.

Maybe it is valid that the release of such high-profile offenders are subject to intense media scrutiny, but what I struggle with is the degree to which women offenders are unfairly targeted in comparison to men. Gay Oakes was confronted a few weeks prior to Christmas by a photographer, who after receiving a tip-off staked out the place where Gay collects her mail. She was, quite rightly and as you or I would be, distinctly unimpressed at having her privacy invaded and did not feel inclined to smile as requested. Consequently a very unflattering photo of her appeared in the *Sunday Star-Times* a week or so later, blown up to take up a considerable amount of room on the page. Why the publication of the photo and why was it blown up? Because those publishing the paper knew it was something we, the community, would want to see.

And so the country is reminded what Gay looks like and who she is and Gay faces another hurdle on what is already an uphill climb as she seeks to respond positively to the chance she has been given by the Parole Board to move her life on beyond the circumstances that led her to prison and to impact in a positive way on the lives of her children

In the end, it comes down to what we, you and I, want. An article in the *Dominion Post* on 3 October 2002 was headlined 'New prisons to cost $400m' and talked about the fact that the previous day when appearing before Parliament's law and order select committee, Corrections Department Chief Executive Mark Byers had stated that four new regional prisons, housing 1400 inmates, will cost about $400 million to build. The article also revealed that the estimated cost of the prison being built at Ngawha in Northland was now $105 million with 'about $1.5 million' having been spent on unexpected legal fees after those objecting to the proposed location of the prison took legal action against the department's decision to build at Ngawha.

As I read, I thought about the children who have died in recent times at the hands of those who are supposed to love and protect them and about the children who are now serving terms of imprisonment after being involved in the senseless and violent murder of another human being and wondered at the degree to which we are getting it wrong.

We can blame parents and social agencies, we can blame the media and politicians, but it seems that in the end it comes down to us, you and me, and whether we are brave enough to admit the part we all play in the loss of the magic from children's lives in this country. It's not about the establishment of a Families Commission to promote the interests of families; it's not about having yet another inquiry into why Kiwi kids are killing and being killed. It's about community building, about turning the cities and towns within New Zealand into villages within which we all play a part in caring for our more vulnerable citizens.

To borrow a line from a review of this book that featured in the *North and South* magazine in September 2002; 'It's three years before you'll get another chance to deliver a considered opinion on these issues: your time starts now.'